THE
Archive Photographs
SERIES

AROUND
YEOVIL

HENRY STIBY, born: 19 January 1843 Sherborne, died: 19 January 1934 Yeovil. Amateur photographer, ironmonger, Sunday school superintendent, hospital vice-president, Woborn Almshouse trustee, 'Children's Friend', Mayor of Yeovil, Justice of the Peace, Alderman, Freeman and museum benefactor (firearms and coins) – Henry Stiby was all of these (and more besides!) in his long life. However, it is to the former that this book pays belated tribute (see Introduction).

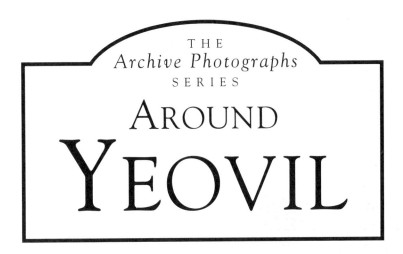

THE
Archive Photographs
SERIES

AROUND

YEOVIL

Compiled by
Robin Ansell and Marion Barnes

CHALFORD

First published 1995
Copyright © Robin Ansell and Marion Barnes, 1995

The Chalford Publishing Company
St Mary's Mill, Chalford,
Stroud, Gloucestershire, GL6 8NX

ISBN 0 7524 0178 5

Typesetting and origination by
The Chalford Publishing Company
Printed in Great Britain by
Redwood Books, Trowbridge

Front cover illustration: Princes Street, *c.* 1900 (see p.28 and p.49).

This book is affectionately dedicated to our respective spouses, Bernie Ansell and Ian Budgett, without whose support it would never have seen the light of day!

HENRY STIBY (1843-1934) AND FRIENDS, *c.* 1885. Amongst his numerous charitable acts, Henry Stiby served for a time as superintendent of Christ Church Sunday School. Known as 'The Children's Friend', he is to be seen here, third from the right, in the back row. The group is thought to be assembled outside the church (Reformed Episcopalian), which opened in The Park in 1880. Built to accommodate 500 worshippers, dwindling numbers led to its untimely demolition in 1904. [Stiby photograph]

Contents

Acknowledgements

The Museum of South Somerset, administered by South Somerset District Council, is located in the old coach house of Hendford Manor, Yeovil. It is actively collecting photographs of the local area and would welcome the opportunity of acquiring or copying any interesting prints you may have. With this in mind we would like to say a special thank you to Michael Shorter ARPS, our photographer, who has produced all the copy prints and negatives for us often at short notice; without his help and expert professional advice the project would have been very difficult indeed.

We would also like to express our thanks to the many people who have given photographs to the museum in the past, and more recently, thereby contributing to this volume.

The authors would like to express their appreciation to the following individuals, who, at various times during its compilation, offered help, advice, information and/or photographs: Master J.T.L. Ansell, Mr R. Ballam, Mr D.A. Bayliss, Mr S.M. Boon, Mr A.J. Boucher, Mr R.D. Brewer, Mr A.J. Brisley, Mr L.E.J. Brooke, Mrs J. Card, Mr M.G. Chant, Dr G. Chapman, Mr & Mrs H. Clark, Mrs A. Clements, Mr C.E.B. Clive-Ponsonby-Fane, Mr L.J. Clotworthy, Mr D. A. Crossland, Mrs P. Cudmore, Mr C.F. Dorey, Mr W.M. Drower, Mr R. Duckworth, Mr D. Foot, Mr E.M. Garrett, Mrs E. Gerrish, Miss E. Glass, Mrs B. Goodchild, Miss J. Gray, Mrs K. Gurnett, Ms E.M. Hebditch, Mr J.A. Hebditch, Mr M.S. Hebditch, Rev D.J. Hunt, Mrs L.M. Jewels, Mr N.G.P. Kibby, Mrs P.A. Knight, Mr & Mrs K. Lane, Mrs B. Langdon, Rev M.E. Laurie, Mr P. Lawson-Clarke, Dr P.S. Luffman, Mr G. Masters, Mr F.J. Matthews, Mr and Mrs R. Matthews, Mr P.J. Moncrieff, Mr B. Moore, Mr E.T.A. Palmer, Mrs M. Partridge, Mr D.R. Phillips, Mr & Mrs H.C. Prudden, Cdr & Mrs S. Radley, Mrs D.C. Robson, Mr B. Rousell, Miss T. Rowe, Miss A.E.A. Shepherd, Mr G. Smith, Mr T. Stok, Mr J.W. Sweet, Mr D.R. Swetman, Mrs & Mrs H.T. Swetman, Mrs P.A. Tupman, Mrs M. Tyler, Mr B. White, Mrs J. Wickes, Mrs B. Williams.

Additionally, the staff of the following organisations have been most helpful: Dorchester Local Studies Library, National Motor Museum (Beaulieu), Sherborne Museum, Sherborne Town Council, South Somerset District Council, Taunton Local History Library, Yeovil Crematorium, Yeovil Register Office, Yeovil Town Council. A special tribute must be paid to the Yeovil Local History Library (Charles Tite Collection). Its comprehensive holdings of *Kelly's Directory of Somerset* (1861-1939), *Whitby's Almanack* (1878-1918), local census returns (1841-1891) and the *Sherborne Mercury/Western Flying Post/Western Gazette* (1737-present) – the latter two on microfilm – have proved invaluable in researching the captions for this book.

WHITBY'S ALMANACK, 1881

Introduction

In January 1839 the Frenchman Louis Jacques Mandé Daguerre (1787-1851) and an Englishman William Henry Fox Talbot (1800-1877), almost simultaneously (and totally independently) announced to an unsuspecting world their respective inventions of photography. Though the 'daguerreotype' was somewhat short-lived, lasting barely twenty years, Talbot's 'photogenic drawing' (and subsequently his 'calotype') was to lead directly to the creation of the modern negative-positive process.

It is interesting to note that Talbot was a local man, having been born at Melbury House, Melbury Sampford, in Dorset – some half-a-dozen miles south of Yeovil! His maternal grandfather was the second Earl of Ilchester (1747-1802). However, most of his pioneering work in photography was undertaken at his ancestral home in Wiltshire – Lacock Abbey, near Chippenham (now owned by the National Trust).

In Yeovil one of the earliest known practitioners of this new art form was a certain 'Mr M. Brown, the celebrated photographic artist' – whose trade advertisement appeared in the *Western Flying Post*, 18 March 1856. His 'Collodion Portrait Rooms' were located 'at Mr Perry's, South Street', though families could be 'waited upon at their own residences'. Portraits were available between '10am till dusk' and were priced from '1s to Two Guineas' each! By the end of April Mr Brown was respectfully tendering 'his thanks to the Clergy, Gentry, and Inhabitants of Yeovil and its Vicinity, for the very liberal patronage they have honoured him with...' It would seem that early Victorian Yeovilians had enthusiastically welcomed the advent of photography to their town!

Other early local 'photographic artists' included: Thomas Sydenham Swatridge, Princes Street (1858); G.M. Hand, Silver Street (1859); Frederick Treble, Sherborne Road (1861) and John Chaffin, Hendford (1862).

However, Adam Gosney (1844-1921) is the earliest commercial photographer about whom much is known and whose work is represented in the following pages. Born in Sherborne, the son of a labourer, his advertisements stated that his photographic business was established in 1866 – though this date probably refers only to the commencement of his Sherborne operation. At various times during a long career, spanning some fifty years, he had studios in: Sherborne, Yeovil, Gillingham, Shaftesbury, Frome, Crewkerne, Dorchester, Wimborne and Wells. By 1881 he was employing three assistants at his Sherborne studio, in Half Moon Street, and 'carte-de-visite' portraits were costing 'from 6s per doz'. Gosney appears to have been a highly active individual around his native town, also being well known for organising firework displays at local shows, and eventually succumbing to his final illness whilst attending a carnival committee meeting.

Nationally, photography was taken up by a growing band of amateurs. They came from all walks of life: the landed gentry, retired army officers, clergymen, artists, writers... and, locally, an ironmonger by the name of Henry Stiby (1843-1934).

Coincidentally, Stiby – like Gosney – was also born in Sherborne, though he came of farming stock. In his younger days he had run the family farm at Stalbridge, in Dorset, but subsequently abandoned the land for the ironmongery business – settling in Yeovil in 1869. From then until 1895 he was in partnership with Thomas Denner (1840?-1912) running an agricultural implement and ironmongers shop, Denner & Stiby, in the High Street.

However, from about 1880 to 1900 he practised the art of photography in his leisure time, taking numerous pictures of local manor houses, churches, follies and friends – in addition to Yeovil street scenes. Fortunately for us his work (though probably only a fraction of his total output) is now permanently preserved at the Museum of South Somerset, in Yeovil – administered by South Somerset District Council and under the curatorial care of Marion Barnes. The Stiby Photographic Collection comprises over thirty original prints (often dated and signed in Stiby's neat copperplate hand) and more than fifty glass-plate negatives. Some of the latter have been especially printed out for this publication.

Stiby was a man of many parts, also interesting himself in such diverse subjects as the church, the blind, youth organisations, animal welfare, astronomy, microscopy and numismatics (to name but a few!). He also managed to find time to serve on numerous public bodies, and was elected Mayor of Yeovil in 1904, Alderman in 1907 and Freeman in 1926 – the first person to be so honoured. On the occasion of receiving the Freedom of the Borough, he thanked the Council with the following words: 'Anything I have done for Yeovil, has been done freely and willingly, and I regard it as instalments of a great debt of gratitude, the full extent of which I shall never be able to pay' – rare modesty indeed!

He never married, and died in Yeovil, on his ninety-first birthday. However, his memory lives on in a road name (Stiby Road) and his precious photographic legacy – a small part of which is reproduced in the following pages.

Robin Ansell and Marion Barnes

[Note: Gosney and Stiby photographs are identified with the relevant captions]

One

Street Scenes

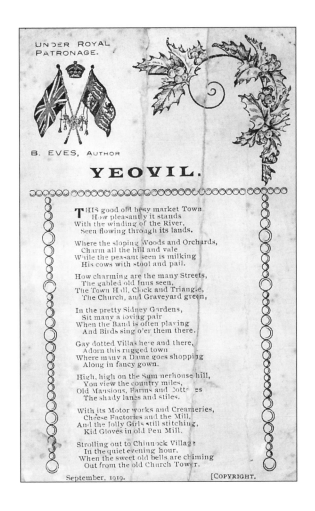

UNDER ROYAL
PATRONAGE.

B. EVES, AUTHOR

YEOVIL.

THIS good old busy market Town,
   How pleasantly it stands
With the winding of the River,
   Seen flowing through its lands.

Where the sloping Woods and Orchards,
   Charm all the hill and vale
While the peasant seen is milking
   His cows with stool and pail.

How charming are the many Streets,
   The gabled old Inns seen,
The Town Hall, Clock and Triangle,
   The Church, and Graveyard green,

In the pretty Sidney Gardens,
   Sit many a loving pair
When the Band is often playing
   And Birds sing o'er them there.

Gay dotted Villas here and there,
   Adorn this rugged town
Where many a Dame goes shopping
   Along in fancy gown.

High, high on the Summerhouse hill,
   You view the country miles,
Old Mansions, Farms and Cottages
   The shady lanes and stiles.

With its Motor works and Creameries,
   Cheese Factories and the Mill,
And the Jolly Girls still stitching,
   Kid Gloves in old Pen Mill.

Strolling out to Chinnock Village
   In the quiet evening hour,
When the sweet old bells are chiming
   Out from the old Church Tower.

September, 1919.   [COPYRIGHT.

AERIAL VIEW OF YEOVIL, *c.* 1945. On the right is the parish church of St. John the Baptist, constructed between 1380-1405, to replace an earlier structure of Saxon origin. It was partly financed by funds that had accrued in previous years from market tolls, and partly through a bequest of the rector, Canon Robert de Sambourne (1334?-1382). Known as 'The Lantern of the West', on account of its impressively large windows, it remains to this day the crowning glory of a town somewhat bereft of architectural treasures! Parish registers survive from 1563

and are now deposited at the Somerset Record Office, Taunton. Also clearly visible, top left, is the Odeon Cinema (1937), Court Ash, which subsequently changed to Cannon and is now operated by MGM (see p.78). Below it, at bottom left, is the 'art deco' Central Cinema (1931), Church Street – sadly demolished to make way for new offices! This photograph was probably taken on market day – judging by the number of trucks parked at the cattle market (top centre).

HENDFORD HILL *c.* 1905. Hendford Supply Stores was one of only four sub post offices in Yeovil in 1906. Its address was 1 Aldon Terrace and the sub-postmaster was George Francis Maidment. The building in the foreground is the Railway Hotel (see p.85), at 24 Hendford, built after the railway opened at nearby Hendford Halt in 1853. The publican at the time this photo was taken was James Charles Dennett.

HENDFORD MANOR *c.* 1914, from a postcard sent in 1914. The manor house on the left, was built in 1750 for James Hooper, and enlarged in the nineteenth-century by Edwin Newman, it is now the offices of Kiddsons Impey chartered accountants. The entrance visible by the street light leads up to Petter's Way car park, the Octagon Theatre, and the manor's coach house now the home of the Museum of South Somerset. The dwellings on the right have been demolished and replaced by office accommodation and the Homeville flats.

VIEW TOWARDS PENN HILL, *c.* 1880. Looking down Hendford Hill, towards the junction with Brunswick Street, the walls on either side of the road form the parapets of the bridge over the Taunton to Yeovil Town railway line (now a foot- and cycle-path). Note the unspoilt beauty of Penn Hill, in the distance, long before the construction of Maltravers House (1969) and the Johnson Hall/Octagon Theatre (1974). [Gosney photograph]

VIEW FROM PENN HILL, *c.* 1880. This panoramic shot was taken from approximately where Maltravers House stands today. In the foreground, left, seen faintly through the trees, is the Hendford Manor (see p.12) coach house – now the home of the Museum of South Somerset. To the right of the tallest tree, is the distinctive roof-line of Hendford House (now the Manor Hotel). Over the roof-tops beyond is the empty field that eventually became the ground of Yeovil Town Football Club (see p.94). Note, at the extreme right, the recently opened Reformed Episcopalian church (1880), in The Park (see p.4). [Gosney photograph]

THE BOROUGH. Above is the left-half of a stereoscopic photograph, dating from around 1860 – the earliest image in this book! The imposing, double-fronted, three-storey building, built in 1856 for the Wilts. & Dorset Bank, is now a branch of Lloyds. In the distance, on the left, is the Town Hall (1849) – minus its clock tower (not erected until 1864). Below, the same scene some 60 years later, looks remarkably similar, apart from the automobile outside the bank. The Town Hall clock tower had previously been declared unsafe, in 1887, and removed. By 1913 it had been re-erected and remained in situ until the building was destroyed by fire in 1935 (see p.85). The tall tree on the left, marks the approximate site of the future King George Street (1928).

THE BOROUGH, *c*. 1914. This part of the town has long been referred to as 'The Borough' and was indeed the centre of the old medieval borough. However, it has never been a proper postal address, being simply a part of the High Street. In the nineteenth-century it was the site of the Market House and Butchers' Shambles, until they were swept away in 1849 following the opening of the new Town Hall (seen here in the distance). The businesses, visible behind the covered stalls, are, left to right: Hill, Sawtell, 15 High Street (ironmongers, heating, sanitary and agricultural engineers); Bray & Sons, 16 High Street (tailors); Carpet & Linoleum Warehouse, 17 High Street; Central Supply Stores, 18 High Street (grocers, tea dealers, provision merchants and suppliers of wines, spirits and Bass, Devenish and Whitbread ales and stouts); James Harold Llewellyn, 20 High Street (fruiterer). Royal proclamations, announcing the accession of a new monarch, have traditionally been read, by the mayor, in The Borough (see p.75 and p.79).

WAR MEMORIAL, THE BOROUGH. On Friday July 16 1917, at a meeting in the Town Hall, the Mayor Alderman Edmund Damon (see p.100) established in principle the need for a war memorial to be erected to honour Yeovil's fallen heroes. Four years later, at 6.00 pm on Thursday July 14 1921, a memorial cross was unveiled by Colonel Frank Davidson Urwick D.S.O. (see p.77). The style and site of the cross was the subject of much debate and a committee had been elected to co-ordinate the project. The end result was designed by Wilfred C. Childs and sculpted by Messrs. Appleby and Childs. The 'Eleanor' style cross, in Ham stone, stands 29 feet high and is hexagonal in plan. A total of 226 names are inscribed on six panels on the lowest tier. The memorial cost £1,250 to construct and takes its name from the wife of Edward I (1239-1307). [Eleanor of Castile had died in Grantham in 1290 and these beautiful crosses were erected by the king at the twelve places that her body rested on its way to Westminster for burial.] The top photograph dated *c*. 1925 shows the Midland Bank at the junction of Borough and Silver Street. The bottom photograph *c*. 1930 sites the cross outside William Redwood tailor and clothiers.

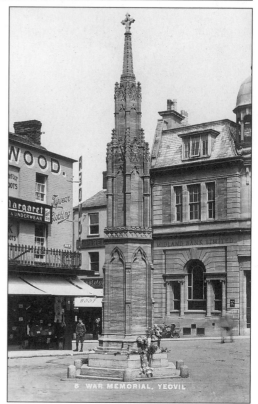

THE CASTLE HOTEL, MIDDLE STREET *c.* 1890. Middle Street was once the site of the Castle Hotel, a medieval building, originally the White Hart, then the Higher Three Cups. From 1768 it was known as the Castle Inn which it remained until 1924 when the building was demolished. This photograph illustrates how narrow the roadway was with barely enough room for a single horse-drawn vehicle. The publican, John Wilkins, was first listed in Kelly's in 1889 – the approximate date of this picture. Joseph Frisby, boot maker had his premises opposite at 111 Middle Street.

MIDDLE STREET, *c.* 1935. A later view of Middle Street with Frisby's shoe store now halfway down on the left. The sign for the New Inn (later the Flying Machine, see p.56) is at the corner of Bond Street and Middle Street now the site of the Nationwide Building Society. Middle Street was pedestrianised in 1971

THE GEORGE HOTEL *c.* 1900. No book of Yeovil and its environs would be complete without a photograph of the fifteenth-century, half-timbered, Wealden style, George Hotel in Middle Street. Built as a private house for a local merchant it became the Three Cups Inn in 1642 and the George Hotel early in the nineteenth-century, Louisa Vincent was the licensee at the George around the turn of the century.

SITE OF THE GEORGE HOTEL *c.* 1965. The former projection of the hotel is the key to its demise. A fatal pedestrian accident at that narrow spot necessitated the road widening which was to follow. The George was demolished amid much public condemnation in 1962, but, as history was to record, this section of Middle street was pedestrianised less than ten years later in 1971. The tall building in the photograph, at the junction of Middle and Union streets, was the former Post Office from 1902-1932 (see p. 45) – now the site of W.H.Smiths.

MIDDLE STREET, *c*. 1900. This photograph of Middle Street looking west was taken around 1900. Membury's at 100 Middle Street was a hairdresser and dealer in fancy goods. Across the street at number 17 was the Albany Temperance Hotel (formerly Coffee Tavern). It is not listed as a public house nor did it need a licensee as it was an alcohol-free establishment. It was run by Alderman Mitchelmore who also operated the Fernleigh Hotel, at 67 Middle Street (see p.20 and p.101).

MIDDLE STREET *c*. 1960. The large double-fronted building at the bottom of the street housed the gas works, built on the site of a drained withy bed in 1833. This entire site is now pedestrian access only and in 1969, two blocks to the right of the gas works were demolished for the erection of the new Tesco's supermarket, replacing the one higher up Middle Street (see p. 56).

MIDDLE STREET *c.* 1930. Central Road is now off to the left in this photograph and Sherborne Road with the cluster of houses in the distance, known to locals as 'take away alley', is straight ahead. The road on the right beyond the railings now leads to old station car park and the large building with the wrought iron balcony is presently Palmers' fish and chip shop, formerly the Fernleigh Commercial Hotel.

VIEW FROM SUMMERHOUSE HILL, *c.* 1950. Penn Hill can be seen in the middle left of this postcard view dominated by Penn House (see p.25). In the foreground is Victoria Bridge crossing the railway line and what is now the Ninesprings cycle-path. There is a small terrace of cottages visible also in the foreground running off to the right. These are known as Victoria Buildings and were used as low cost accommodation for those people employed in the gloving industry. By the time this photograph was taken the gloving trade was in the doldrums. What had started as a general decline just after the war, was to accelerate into a catastrophic disaster and from a peak of twenty-five gloving companies operating in the 1930s, the last one in Yeovil closed in 1989.

SUMMERHOUSE TERRACE, *c*. 1960. Summerhouse Terrace, from the junction with Stars Lane, shortly before it was demolished to make way for a car park. The date stone of 1876 is visible between two upstairs windows.

SUMMERHOUSE TERRACE (CAR PARK) *c*. 1960. Above is the resulting car park, viewed from the site of Summerhouse Terrace. This development also claimed another victim, Talbot Street, which ran parallel with and behind Summerhouse Terrace. Demolished to accommodate increased demand for parking, at the time time this photograph was taken it may be argued that the end did not justify the means!

SOUTH STREET *c.* 1958.
South Street was known in much
earlier times as 'Back Street', as it
marked the boundary of the
medieval borough. The Yeovil
Community Arts Centre, which
opened in 1988, occupies the
building on the right hand side of
the top picture. At 80 South Street
it once housed a doctor's surgery as
did the house next door which was
eventually demolished and is now
the adjoining car park. 79 South
Street was the home of physician
Ptolemy Samuel Henry Colmer
(1840-1897), Mayor of Yeovil from
1887-1889 and 1890-1892. The
1881 census lists Dr. Colmer, his
wife and six children, as well as his
sister and four domestic servants all
residing at the same address!

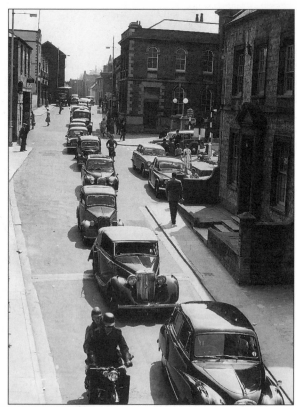

The congestion of cars in both
pictures is clearly visible, often
necessitating a policeman with
white gloves on point duty. At the
corner of South Street and Petter's
Way is the Baptist church (see
p.70).

SOUTH STREET, 12 November 1955. Two school boys are obviously fascinated by the road reconstruction happening around them at the bottom of South Street. The building just in front of W.J. Glossop's lorry and opposite Union Street is the old Hendford Parish School demolished in 1965. The school was built in 1862 to accommodate 200 girls and 200 infants.

THE GREYHOUND HOTEL, SOUTH STREET, 21 January 1956. The building on the left was once the old Cheese Market, converted into the Yeovil Volunteer Fire Brigade Offices and Station in 1913. In 1962 they moved to purpose-built premises at Reckleford, allowing the old site to be redeveloped eventually as part of the new Yeovil Library, which opened in 1987. The Greyhound Hotel shown here replaced an earlier construction of the same name (see p.70).

PETER STREET. This leafy thoroughfare of 1968 (above), named after Peter Daniell (see opposite), is hardly recognisable today – until you look, below, at the same scene the following year! The onslaught of the post-war developer was well-advanced by this time, increasing the 'acreage' under car parks at an alarming rate. One of these early nineteenth-century properties (no.7), was once rented by the novelist Thomas Hardy (1840-1928). He lived here, between March and July 1876, prior to settling in Sturminster Newton, Dorset. His former residence in Yeovil is now marked, not by a 'blue plaque', but by a 'pay-and-display' ticket-machine!

MILL LANE, *c*. 1960. This photograph, shows the location of Woodland Terrace on Mill Lane. This lane ran from the southern end of Summerhouse Terrace west into Addlewell Lane. Frog Mill was situated at the lower end and is recorded in the Domesday book (1086) as being worth 10s. A disastrous fire in 1909 (see p.82) all but destroyed Chapman's mill and after a variety of uses, the water wheel and sluice gate disappeared under new roadworks, linking Summerhouse Terrace and Park Street.

PENN HOUSE, PENN HILL, October 1968. This imposing late eighteenth-century, Ham stone house, set amid extensive grounds, once dominated Penn Hill (see p.20). However, its isolated position has gradually been encroached upon, over the intervening years, by residential development. One of its earliest owners was Peter Daniell (1764-1834), a prosperous mercer, town developer and commanding officer of the local volunteer infantry – and after whom Peter Street (see opposite) was named.

GEORGE COURT, 1931. George Court formerly ran from High Street to South Street and was once the courtyard of a seventeenth-century inn called The George. It ceased to be an inn around the end of the eighteenth-century and by 1846 the court carried quite an unsavoury reputation. It was eventually purchased by the Town Council, to enable King George Street to be built as a link between High Street and South Street, completed in 1928.

CORN EXCHANGE, April 1962. Yeovil's corn exchange was built at the same time as the imposing Town Hall (see p. 85), on the South Side of the High Street in 1849. The site provided much needed space for the conducting of market business and administration, most of which had previously been confined to the Borough. The new complex of buildings stretched from the High Street frontage of the Town Hall to South Street at the rear and included a meat market, corn exchange(shown here being demolished) and a cheese and bacon room with a flax chamber over the top.

VICARAGE STREET. The parish church of St. John the Baptist (see p.10 and p.11), dominates both of these images, despite them being some 70 years apart. Right, around 1900, the nearest building is also a church – belonging to the Unitarians. It traced its origins back to the mid seventeenth-century, though this particular place of worship dated only from 1704. During the nineteenth-century it was rebuilt at least twice. At the far end of the dwellings, on the left, was a long, narrow, tapering shed that had housed the Yeovil Volunteer Fire Brigade since 1861. They moved to better premises, on South Street, in 1913 (see p.23). Below, Percy Winsor (1893?-1972), extended his agricultural engineering business into the now redundant adjoining Unitarian church. However, by the time this photograph was taken, about 1970, his premises were empty and up for sale. Note that the street has now become one-way only, the ubiquitous double-yellow lines have appeared and the buildings, on the left, have been demolished – as evidenced by the shadows on the tarmac!

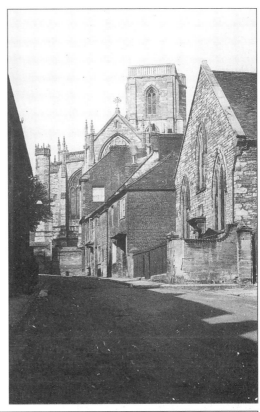

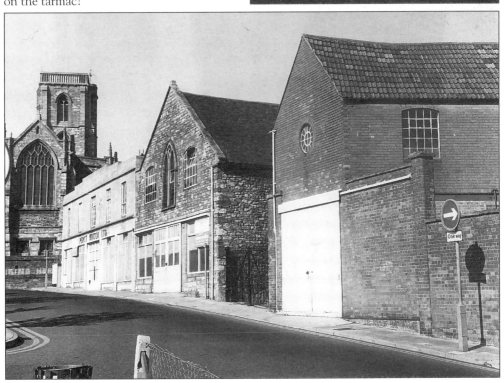

HENDFORD. An interesting 'then-and-now' sequence, separated by some 75 years. Above, looking along Hendford towards its junction with Princes Street, High Street and Porter's Lane (now Westminster Street), around 1895. The absence of the Capital & Counties Bank (1897), on the corner of Princes/High streets helps to date this photograph. (This cross-roads is also featured, some five years later, on the front cover of this book). Below, is the same scene, about 1970, when the traffic problems of the town had become a little more acute – and the man with his paint brush had daubed double-yellow lines almost everywhere! Note, however, the surprising similarities: the Three Cloughs Hotel has merely sprouted sun-blinds and a canopy; Newton's the chemists seems to have been in a 'time-warp' over the intervening years!

PRINCES STREET, *c.* 1930. The large shop front with elegant pillars is Albion House, better known since 1844 as Whitby's stationers and booksellers. The building at the far end of the terrace is Old Sarum House, built in about 1730 by Samuel Dampier. It was the former home of John Ryall Mayo (1793-1870) who was the first Mayor of Yeovil in 1854.

PRINCES STREET, *c.* 1970. Looking towards Denners 40 years later, the increase in traffic is obvious. Many family stores have long since disappeared including Trelawney's dress shop just visible on the left hand side of this picture, and 'Soyers of Yeovil' next door, advertised as 'Fish merchants, Poulterers and Game dealers'. They also had premises at 73 Middle Street and in addition claim to have provided fruit, flowers and frozen foods, English and Continental.

KINGSTON, *c*. 1920. In this somewhat empty view of Kingston, the Red Lion Hotel, licensee Charles Brown, can be seen on the right just beyond the trees in Bide's Gardens (see p.32). Next door to the pub, identifiable by the flag-pole, is the Yeovil County School (see p.88). Children attending the school used to patronise Horniblow's, the 'unofficial' tuck shop, on the opposite side of the road. Whether the Red Lion fulfilled a similar function for the masters is not recorded! The boy cyclist looks to be headed for the former, or is he just late for school? Notable amongst its 'Old Boys' were the author Walter Raymond (see p.96) and Professor Alfred John Sutton Pippard (1891-1969), president of the Institution of Civil Engineers, 1958-1959. The school's motto was: 'Esse quam videri' – 'To be rather than to seem'. Note the postman on his rounds, wearing a shako-style hat (see p.45), laden down with parcels. He appears to have stopped on the pavement, in front of this attractive row of villas, for a chat with an unseen resident. A photographer attempting to take a similar view today, would be faced with the daunting prospect of standing in the middle of a busy dual-carriageway!

COURT ASH *c.* 1960. Looking towards Vincents in the 1960's this road leads down to the cinema, built on the site of the earlier Court Ash House, which gave its name to the road. Vincents car showroom was built in 1928 by Stanley Howard Vincent. (see p. 79)

FIVEWAYS, August 1967. This view of Fiveways, looking towards Kingston is almost unrecognisable today. The terraced buildings visible just passed the milk float are the only part of this scene still identifiable in the present road layout. The roundabout looks more like a mini roundabout by today's standards, and the light in the centre was a thoughtful addition.

BIDE'S GARDENS, *c.* 1930. An earlier view of the intersection (see p.31) taken in the late 1920's. The grounds of Kingston Manor were bequeathed to the Town by Thomas William Dampier-Bide (1844-1916) and became known as Bide's Gardens. The Georgian manor house became a nursing home attached to a new Yeovil general hospital built in the manor grounds. The house was finally demolished when the present district hospital was completed in 1973.

BIDE'S GARDENS, *c.* 1968. The new maternity unit seen here opened in 1968, five years before the new district hospital. The remains of Bide's Gardens straddle the footpath but were eventually lost with the extension of Reckleford from The Avenue to Princes Street. The sole remaining vestiges are the grass verge with trees between Court Ash and Reckleford and the greensward in front of the maternity wing.

WELLINGTON STREET, September 1957. A view looking towards Yeovil's first National School, on Huish, opened in 1846. These mid nineteenth-century terraces, named after the Duke of Wellington (1769-1852), were demolished soon after this photograph was taken – to make way for the Wellington House flats. The area behind the school has recently undergone redevelopment, with the demolition of the Yeovil Town Football Club ground (see p.94), and the construction of a new Tesco superstore.

HUISH, c. 1900. Looking along Huish, these attractive mid nineteenth-century terraces are bisected by Queen Street. The shop at the junction, advertising 'Fry's Chocolate', was immediately opposite Charles Lane's 'off-licence', and grocers (see p.60). Behind the brick wall, on the left, was the old fair ground. Huish takes its name from the Anglo-Saxon word 'hiwisc' – meaning 'homestead'.

DANIELSFIELD ROAD. This 'classic' inter-war development off East Coker Road took the form of bungalows with fairly large frontages, on a private road. The top photograph was taken in November 1961, looking south towards Turners Barn Lane. The photograph below, taken in July 1962, shows the extent of the road reconstruction. No longer a private road, the large building on the right in the lower picture housed for many years, Hendford Halt, a shop specialising in model railways.

STIBY ROAD. Looking towards Ilchester Road, from Westfield Grove, the above view was taken 8 June 1955. There was no vehicular access to Ilchester Road from Stiby Road until the late 1960s and the trees that can be seen on the right hand side were cleared away when the developers moved in to construct the Southway Drive estate. The photograph below of Ilchester Road, with Stiby Road cornered by Hide Farm, is dated 7 September 1956.

MILFORD ROAD, March 1956. This steep descent from Goldcroft is popularly known as 'Milford Dip'. St George's Avenue, is visible on the left and allotments now take up the area in front. Opposite the Avenue is Melrose Road, with what appears to be scrub land in front, now the site of a playing field.

PRESTON ROAD/ LARKHILL ROAD, c. 1970. Larkhill Lane, as it was known, used to be the dividing line between the parishes of Preston Plucknett (left) and the Borough of Yeovil (right). Preston was absorbed into Yeovil in 1928 when boundary extensions incorporated the village into the borough.

Two

Industries

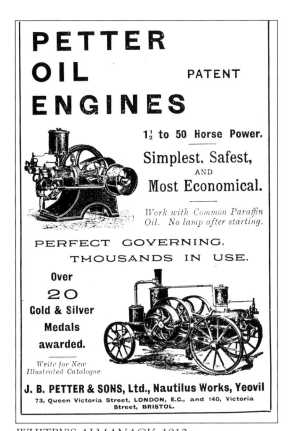

WHITBY'S ALMANACK, 1910

GLOVE FACTORIES, c. 1925. This view from atop Summerhouse Hill, illustrates several of the thirty-plus glove manufacturers operating in the town. The three-storey building in the foreground, wedged between Summerhouse Terrace (see p.21) and Dodham Brook (see p.39), was Blake & Fox – whose appropriate telegraphic address was 'Foxglove'! To the left of the tall chimney, also in the foreground and somewhat obscured by trees, was Ebenezer Pittard's (see p.99) Mill Lane dressing yard. Behind the Coronation Hotel (see p.57), identifiable by the distinctive white-trimmed gables, centre right, was Whitby's large Middle Street factory.

CLOTHIER, GILES GLOVE FACTORY, c. 1930. In the foreground is Walter Jukes (see p.113), working with other 'beamsmen' in the 'unhairing' department of this Addlewell Lane glove factory. Facing towards the natural light, afforded by the windows, men would stoop to use their curved 'unhairing' knives to produce the required smooth skins. These were subsequently submerged in large lime pits and allowed to soak for up to a month. Needless to say, the work was both smelly and back-breaking – and long before health and safety legislation!

UNEMPLOYED GLOVERS CLEARING OUT DODHAM BROOK, *c.* 1930. Herbert George 'Bert' Jukes (see p.113), at top left holding a spade handle, is enjoying a rare spell of sunshine and fresh air with his fellow workers. At times when the gloving industry was in recession, useful work like flood prevention provided temporary alternative employment. It is alleged that some of the Barwick Park follies were constructed in similar circumstances (see p. 105).

THRING & LUFFMAN, *c.* 1910. This office photograph shows Sidney Theodore Thring (1873?-1946) on the left, and Reginald John Luffman (1880?-1961) – partners in the well-known glove manufacturers located at 64 Reckleford. Mr Thring, a native of Milborne Port, was president of the Yeovil and District Glove Manufacturers' Association. Mr Luffman, a Yeovilian and a keen sportsman, was once offered the chance to play for Aston Villa Football Club – but turned it down, since he did not want to lose his amateur status!

NAUTILUS WORKS, RECKLEFORD, c. 1955. James Bazeley Petter's invention of the 'nautilus' grate gained royal approval when Queen Victoria ordered one for Osborne House and Balmoral. It also launched the company, which was to become Westland Helicopters Ltd, in a history which lasted over one hundred years. James' twin sons Ernest and Percy later joined the firm and from 1892, after a spate in pioneering car design, developed a variety of oil engines. In 1902 they produced the first true powered agricultural tractor and in 1910 established James B. Petter & Co. Ltd. as a public company, with a share capital of £150,000. The extensive Nautilus works seen in the top photograph at the corner of Reckleford and Goldcroft included assembly and machine workshops, a packing department and an office block.

PETTERS STAFF, *c.* 1925. Back row, left to right: W.G. Holt, William Austin. Second row: 'Tommy' Bannister, W.J. Poole, H.A. Cornish, Jack W. Hellier, H. Baker. Third row: A.R. Gould, G. Old, H.C. Marsh, G.W. Norris, T.A. Stagg, F. Evans, E.M. Wyatt, Frank Swetman, G. Forsey, G.K. Baguley, A.G. Lichterman. Front: H. White, Fitzherbert Glass (1875-1969), H.S. Saunders, E.P. 'Teddy' Wrinch, J. Booth, A.M. Brown, A.E. Easthope, William H. Farthing, F.W. Holland, H.G. Duncan, T. Pound. The group is believed to be assembled outside the east front of the Mansion House, 42 Kingston (now Princes Street). Note the reflection, in the right window, of the tower belonging to the parish church of St. John the Baptist (see p.10 and p.11).

Opposite: The inside of the works is shown in the bottom photograph. It was also equipped with its own foundry and powerhouse – current for Yeovil's first electric street lamps was supplied by the Petter generating station in 1913. The entire resources of Petters were placed at the government's disposal in 1915 for war work and the manufacture of aircraft began. Petters became part of the Brush group in 1939 and production was transferred to Loughborough. The Nautilus factory and its foundry were closed and the premises became the Southern National bus garage.

WESTLAND AIRCRAFT STAFF (PETTERS DIVISION), 1938. Back row, left to right: -?-, -?-, P. Gould, -?-, R. Davey, -?-, B. Skinner, ? Pyne, -?-, -?-, P. May, C.J. Hockey, -?-, B. Pugsley, T. Dowsett, H.Hitchcock, W. Farthing, ? Langdon, ? Robbins, -?-, J. Dalymont. Second row: W. Baker, -?-, W. Voce, J. Bicknell, H. Gilham, P. Francis, ? Baker, F. Kirby, S. Guy, H. Norris, D. Allen, ? Borman, W. Moulton, H. Williams, H. Langdon, B. Helyar, C. Berry, H. Wakely, -?-, W. May, E. Taverner, J. Hobbs, G. Forsey, W. Webb, -?-, E. Collins, W. Culverhouse. Third row: A. Penny, P.L. Swetman, H.T. Bird, H. Payne, A. Rowse, J. Helyar, -?-, -?-, -?-, J. Foote, P. Pilton, W. Pearce, C. Major, -?-, L.T. Swetman, J. Massie, T. Farwell, ? Webb, J. Hockey, R. Hamblin, -?-, -?-, S. Cupper. Fourth row: -?-, C. Bennett, A. Pike, ? Stone, W. Purchase, B. Warner, W. Lester, A. Brown, D. Trigger, F. Vick, E. Tuck, C. Gale, ? Case, G. Harrison, J. Harrison, F. Harrison, -?-, R. Lukins, A. Stickland, A.H. Francis, C. Parsons, A. Hockey, A. Saunders, G. Vallard, J. Rendall, E. Rendall, -?-, W. Hellier, J. Hulbert, S. Hiscott. Fifth row: G. Gould, -?-, -?-, -?-, B. Priddle, J. Norris, H. Parr, G. Berry, A.C. Hann, E.P. Wrinch, Capt. R.C. 'Dick' Petter, C. Stagg, S. Parr, H. Gale, F. Glass, C. Allen, G. Hellier, W. Webber, G. Hill, ? Meade. Front row: H. Tucker, H. Brooks, W. Rendall, B. Woods, S. Milligan, P. Plowman, L. Pilkington, B. Cox, Miss A. White, -?-, ? Egland, F.W. Tuck, G. Garrett, H. Brown, S. Phillips, M. Hawkins, -?-, -?-, H. Chainey, T. Willey.

Three

Public Services

WHITBY'S ALMANACK, 1883

YEOVIL HOSPITAL, FIVEWAYS. The town's first 'modern' hospital, above and below, was located on the triangle of land between Preston Road and Ilchester Road. Built at a cost of over £1,000 it opened somewhat precipitately, in 1872, amidst a smallpox epidemic. During 1908, the approximate date of both photographs, the hospital had 110 in-patients and 559 out-patients under treatment. With the opening of a new hospital in Bide's Gardens, in 1922, this building became a maternity home. In 1968 a new maternity unit opened (see p.32), also in Bide's Gardens, and Fiveways became redundant. It was demolished the following year. The identities of two of the boys, above, are known: third from the left is William Frank Sweet (1896?-1914). He enlisted in the Somerset Light Infantry at the outbreak of the First World War, but never made it to the Front – dying of pneumonia whilst undergoing initial training on Salisbury Plain. His cousin, fifth from the left, Reginald William Sweet (1899-1989) served with the Wiltshire Regiment and won the MM at Ypres, April 1918. Wounded some six months later, he spent the remainder of his long life in the gloving industry.

POST OFFICE WORKERS *c.* 1910. A group photograph of Yeovil's first postmen outside the Post Office on the corner of Union and Middle streets. Henry Sumsion, allegedly Yeovil's first postman, is standing in the centre front row and is the subject of the vignette. The portrait was taken in September 1918 when he was serving in the Somerset Light Infantry, it shows Henry wearing the uniform issued to wounded soldiers which comprised a light blue jacket and trousers, white shirt and red tie; the soldier's regulation service cap and badge was also worn.

YEOVIL AMBULANCE SECTION 1939. At the outbreak of the Second World War units of ambulance personnel were set up to respond to the realities of war. The main ambulance station was in Salthouse Lane (still identifiable by the large red crosses) and sections were deployed in various locations throughout the town.

YEOVIL BOROUGH COMPANY, HOME GUARD, *c.* 1944. Back row, left to right: Second Lieutenant Leonard J. Crouch, Second Lieutenant Maurice Drummond Stirling, Second Lieutenant John S. Snell, Lieutenant Cyril Jack 'John' Pittard (1908-1987), Second Lieutenant Douglas Wreford Pittard (1904-1989), Second Lieutenant Walter J. Bilby, Second Lieutenant Victor Ball. Front: Lieutenant William Way MM, Captain Walter C. Noble MC, Major Harold Charles Edward Oliver MC, Colonel Herbert Copeland Cary Batten DSO (see p.102), Captain Howard T. Whittaker, Lieutenant W.H. Rawlins, Lieutenant Edwin Charles Snell. In November 1941 the company strength was 369 – with headquarters at Little Aldon. It formed part of the third Somerset (Yeovil) Battalion, whose combined strength was over 3,000. 'Dad's Army' in reality! (The name of the 'mascot' is not known).

Four
Traders

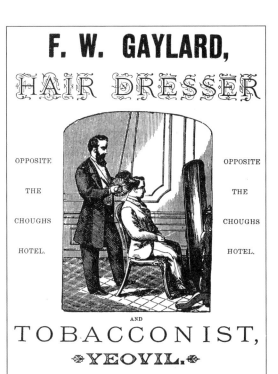

WHITBY'S ALMANACK, 1882

DENNER'S, 79 HENDFORD, c. 1895. It was around 1875 that Linsey Denner (1844-1917), a native of Honiton, Devon, began his drapery business in the town. Some six years later, he was already well-established – employing 12 staff – at 25 High Street (see p.49). By 1890 he had extended his operations, and opened a 'gentleman's and juvenile ready-made and out-fitting establishment' at 79 Hendford, seen above. It is believed that the older figure is Mr Denner, with several of his assistants. Thomas Denner (see p.8) was his brother. To the left of the shop was Stuckey's Bank (now National Westminster Bank) and to the right, Porter's Lane (now Westminster Street). By 1928 these premises had been demolished to make way for the construction of Westminster Street.

DENNER'S, 25 HIGH STREET. The drapery business started, appropriately, in premises that had originally been built for an earlier firm of drapers, Edwards & Dean, in 1836. The building was erected on the site of Yeovil's first known post office. Above is the shop, around 1905, when the adjacent property was occupied by the Rainbow Dye Works, at 1 Hendford. By the time of the second photograph, below, about 1925, Denner's had extended (again!) around the corner into the former dye works. Note that the Sugg gas lamp (see front cover), centre, has 'lost' two of its glass lanterns! It had been presented to the town by he Yeovil Gas and Coke Company, in 1887, to commemorate Queen Victoria's 'golden jubilee'.

HIGH STREET *c.* 1930. Looking towards Huish from the present Cheltenham and Gloucester Building Society. In the distance can be seen Seaton's 'tower' at the junction of Westminster and Clarence streets, the site of which is now included in the Tesco's complex.

GLIDDONS, 3 HIGH STREET *c.* 1960. This photograph shows the extensive front window display of Gliddons fashion store. The business was founded in 1907, next door to the Mermaid Hotel, by John Gliddon. He was followed by his son, another John, who sold off the department store side of the business in 1961. The present store, specialising in sheepskin and leather products, opened in Princes Street shortly after. In the late 1970s Gliddons was granted a royal warrant and now supplies gloves to the Queen.

GLIDDONS MANNEQUIN PARADE, 1925. Fashion shows or 'Mannequin Parades' as they were known were often put on for discerning customers as this photograph above shows. Taken in 1925 at the Assembly Rooms, Yeovil for J. Gliddons, this 'wedding party' is made up of staff and professional models. The staff are Miss Ball (bride), Miss Denslow, Miss Holly (bridesmaids), Miss Sellwood as the end guest. The head dresses were made by Miss Doris Francis. The second photograph, below, was taken at Gliddons on 10 March 1937. The female staff present were: the Misses House, Andrews, Mansfield, Hill, Hobbs, Franklin, Snook, Hooper, Gilham, Close, Irish, Westlake, Ansell, Frost, Akey, Baker and Taylor. At about this time Gliddons were offering a 'model coat in navy fine wove hopsack, trimmed opossum fur collar, with the new four way neckline for 59s 11d' (approximately £3).

HIGH STREET *c.* 1930. Corner of High Street and Hendford, looking up the High Street towards the National Westminster Bank. The horse and cart is just pulling away from the Mermaid Hotel, which dates back to around 1500 and is the oldest established licensed premises still in the town. Barclays Bank visible on the corner is now a soft furnishings store, and the window above was once part of the offices of the former Yeovil Borough Council.

HIGH STREET *c.* 1970. A later view looking the same way towards the junction with Hendford. The fashionable lady waiting at the kerb would date this picture to the early 1970s. The introduction of decimalisation and the impact of space travel was yet to take effect. Perhaps the Moulton bicycle leaning up against Richard Shops is an indication of progress.

THE BOROUGH, 1939. A view of the Borough looking towards the top of Middle Street. Boots the chemist, formerly the Medical Hall, was bombed in April 1941. The damage was so severe that the building was demolished.

WINE VAULTS, UNION STREET c. 1900. The Wine Vaults in Union Street at the junction with Wine Street. Wine Street was once known as gGrope Lane. Mann & Co were wine and spirit merchants. The premises is now owned and run by Bass Ltd. The boy on the corner is posibly a telegraph boy from the nearby Post Office.

THE GLOBE INN, 2 PARK STREET, 12 November 1955. Addlewell Lane is just visible on the left hand side infront of the Globe Inn. The inn which stood at the entrance to Park Street was demolished in the 1960s. This photograph taken at the same time as the photograph on p.23, shows the disruption caused by the reconstruction of the A30 trunk road. The shop on the right hand side is still in use as a fast-food outlet.

W.H. SMITHS, MIDDLE STREET c. 1920. Upper Middle Street looking towards the Borough. The absence of the war memorial dates this picture to pre 1921. The canopies are down in front of the old W.H. Smiths.

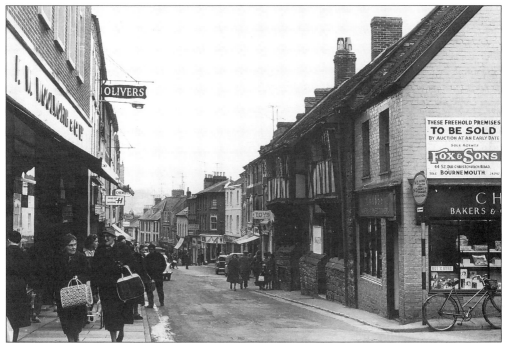

MIDDLE STREET / UNION STREET *c.* 1960. Known as 'Pit Lane' in earlier times because it led to the town's tanning and flax pits, this photograph shows, on the right, the George Hotel and Chubbs, the bakers and confectioners. Note the sign in the window advertising hot cross buns which indicates that this picture was taken at Easter.

TOM COOMBS BAKERY, 69 MIDDLE STREET, *c.* 1975. Starting off as a market trader, Tom Coombs (1878-1964), subsequently established his own bakery, in 1932. After several moves within the town, he settled at 69 Middle Street. Kay Reed is the manageress, and her 'customers' are Valerie Poole and George Puckett. Sadly, the business closed in 1988.

MIDDLE STREET / BOND STREET, *c.* 1975. This 1970s photograph of Yeovil's first Tesco store is instantly dated by the clothes and signage of the period. Tesco was offering double Green Shield stamps and there is not a shopping trolley in sight! Goods purchased were now often taken home by cars parked in one of the prestigious new car parks, like the one below.

VICARAGE STREET (CAR PARK), *c.* 1970. A far cry from today's multi-storey and out of town retail developments. The once familiar car park attendants, with their ticket machines, have now been replaced by car park wardens and separate 'pay-and-display' ticket machines – which do not even give change! The old Unity Hall (Labour Club) is visible in the background, all now under the present Quedam shopping centre.

MIDDLE STREET *c*. 1925. The original Co-op building opened in 1910 and is seen at the top of lower Middle Street. Cars were now a popular mode of private transport and as in this picture often came face to face with horse-drawn carts. The tall building on the right is the Coronation Hotel.

MIDDLE STREET *c*. 1970. The old Co-op building became Hampshire's department store when the new Co-op relocated within Glovers Walk, which opened in 1969. The symbols visible on the top of the original building have now disappeared. The centre one being the old Co-op logo (wheatsheaf and clasped hands).

THE ALEXANDRA HOTEL, 14 SOUTH WESTERN TERRACE, *c.* 1885. Built following the opening of the Town Station (see p.64 and p.65) in 1861, which it overlooked, the hotel was named after Princess Alexandra (1844-1925), future consort of Edward VII (1841-1910). Over the main entrance can be seen the licensee's name 'Chas. Warr' and over the right side-door 'C. Warr's Posting House – Good Stabling' – indicating that accommodation for both two- and four-legged guests was available. Charles Warr, a native of Alvington, ran this establishment throughout the 1880s, at a time when Yeovil could boast of 17 public houses and 40 beer retailers (see p.60) – though the population of the borough was only 8,480! At the extreme right, the property with the pointed roof-line, is the re-sited Penstile Toll House, now Newton Lodge (see p.62). The attractive picket-fence marks the boundary of the station forecourt, upon which the photographer has set his tripod.

VINCENT AND EARLE STREET STORES, *c.* 1970. Standing at the junction of the two roads, this local grocers was typical of those built at the turn of the century to serve the newly developed local communities. Much of Earle Street was demolished for car parking in the early 1970s. This whole area disappeared when the Quedam shopping centre was developed.

THE QUICKSILVER MAIL, HENDFORD HILL, *c.* 1914. This unusual photograph was taken outside the Quicksilver Mail at the top of Hendford Hill. Greyhound racing was a popular pastime in Yeovil, with meets at Larkhill. and other local venues.

BEER RETAILER, 67 QUEEN STREET, *c.* 1900. The gentleman on the doorstep is Charles Lane, a native of North Perrott, who, as the sign above him indicates, was 'licensed to retail beer ale' though 'not to be drunk on the premises'. There were thirty-eight such establishments in Yeovil at this time! Judging by the contents of the well-stocked window, the shop also served as a grocers. Mr Lane was something of a small-scale Victorian entrepreneur, with a tailoring business at 64 Huish as well!

GROCERS, HUISH, July 1964. Dennis George Montague ran the corner shop at 153, Huish and lived next door. The business served the local community with most of the local needs catered for including an on site off-licence. It may be ironic that next door to his house, slightly proud of the terrace, is the Huish Baptist Chapel. Built in 1895, it was enlarged in July 1906, when a school room had been constructed underneath and the over all floor area increased by twenty feet square. The overall enlargement enabled the seating capacity to be duly increased to two hundred and fifty.

Five

Transport

AUTOCAR, 29 October 1926

TOLL HOUSES. The top photograph, dated August 1967, is looking along Kingston towards the junction known as Fiveways (see p. 31). The building on the right is the re-built Kingston Toll House which was moved about a hundred yards from its original position, following the abolition of the Yeovil Turnpike Trust in 1875. At the same time the toll-gates that used to straddle the road at the 'five cross-ways' were removed. The toll house was finally demolished in 1969 for road widening and the building of Yeovil's first district hospital. The lower photograph shows Penstile Toll House, which originally had a 'stop gate near the entrance from Pen Stile to Newton' – hence the name. This house was also re-erected but on the corner of Newton Road, in the mid nineteenth-century.

YEOVIL PEN MILL STATION. Opened 1 September 1856, Pen Mill is the only surviving railway station in the town. Both of these views were taken from the Sherborne Road (A30) over-bridge – but in opposite directions. Looking south, above, around 1925 the tracks veering left lead to Dorchester, via Maiden Newton. In the left foreground are the cattle-pens, where animals from Yeovil market would await transportation. Long-since abandoned, these pens are still visible today, though somewhat overgrown! A solitary locomotive, with 'steam up', waits patiently at the signal-box on the Yeovil Town connecting line (see p.64). The view northwards, below, some 25 years later shows the station proper, with its island-platform. On the name-board it states 'Yeovil Pen Mill change for Durston Branch' – the route to Taunton, via Yeovil Town. The two men beneath the signals are, right, Fred Matterface (yard foreman) and Brian Whittle (telegraph boy). 'In steam' is the yard-shunter and bank-engine – an unidentified 0-6-0 pannier tank. Semaphore signals, similar to those shown here, are still in use – quite a rare survival on the modern Railtrack network! Pen Mill was the site of a major railway accident in 1913 (see p.84).

PEN MILL RAILWAY CUTTING, *c. 1905*. Looking towards Pen Mill, this steam locomotive is hauling its six coaches in the direction of Yeovil Town Station. This connecting line was opened in 1857 and dismantled in the late 1960s. Since then it has been converted, by South Somerset District Council, into a most attractive linear foot- and cycle-path. The River Yeo (Ivel) is seen meandering at the right and the lower slopes of Windmill Hill (now Wyndham Hill) sweep down to the left of the railway track.

YEOVIL TOWN STATION. The Town Station, left and above, opened 1 June 1861, was the last of Yeovil's four railway stations to be built – having been preceded by: Hendford (1 October 1853), Pen Mill (1 September 1856) and the Junction (19 July 1860). It was designed by the architect, Sir William Tite (1798-1873), and possessed two stationmasters and three different staffs – GWR, LSWR and Joint – overmanning in the extreme! In the left view, dated about 1885, the photographer Henry Stiby (see p.2) must have set up his glass-plate camera in the small field in front of South Western Terrace. Note Summerhouse Hill, in the background, from which the photograph on the following double-page spread was taken. Above, of similar date, is the station frontage seen directly along Station Road (now Old Station Road). South Western Terrace, including the Alexandra Hotel (see p.58), is at the left, with William Skinner's coal yard on the right. Yeovil Town Station finally closed 1 March 1967, a victim of the Beeching 'axe', and the buildings were subsequently demolished (see p.69) to make way for yet another car park.

PANORAMIC VIEW OF YEOVIL TOWN STATION, *c.* 1880. An unknown photographer climbed the lower slopes of Summerhouse Hill, to obtain this truly amazing image. A wealth of internal evidence has helped to date this photograph quite precisely. The locomotive, right, quietly waiting in the sidings until called into service, is believed to be a Beattie 0-6-0 of 1876. Note the apparently identical steam-engine, over to the far right, at rest outside the LSWR engine shed. The house-like building, also at the right, located on the bank of Dodham Brook (see p.39) was known as the 'signing-on' shed. In the foreground, above, there is a lower-

quadrant semaphore signal of about 1875. Across the tracks from this signal, there appears to be a pile of discarded iron chairs and baulk timbers, usually associated with broad-gauge – which had been lifted locally by June 1879. Above and behind the early types of engineering wagons, in the GWR goods yard, can be seen the Alexandra Hotel (see p.58). Looming over all, in the background, is Windmill Hill (now Wyndham Hill) topped by its familiar group of lime trees.

LOCOMOTIVE 114 *FROME* (2-2-2 SINGLE-WHEELER), *c.* 1861. A somewhat faded photograph of what is reputedly one of the first locomotives ever to be employed at the Town Station. Built in 1849 by Christie, Adams & Hill, at Thames Bank Ironworks, Rotherhithe, its driving-wheel was 6 feet 6 inches in diameter! On the foot-plate are, left to right: William Greenaway (fireman), Matthew Woods (foreman) and John Knight (driver). The latter, a Yorkshireman, subsequently left the London & South Western Railway to become the licensee of the Half Moon, on Silver Street, later moving to Bradpole, Dorset – to run yet another pub.

LOCOMOTIVE 34052 *LORD DOWDING* (4-6-0 BATTLE OF BRITAIN CLASS), *c.* 1955 This British Railways locomotive, 'snapped' a short distance outside the Town Station, was originally built for the Southern Railway, at Eastleigh, in 1946. Its design is considerably more sleek than the steam-engine in the above photograph! Note the glove factories and the houses on Penn Hill in the background. Summerhouse Hill was certainly an ideal vantage-point for the photographically-inclined 'train-spotter'.

YEOVIL TOWN STATION. An interesting 'before-and-after' sequence, separated by about 20 years. Above, looking from Summerhouse Hill, are the station, engine shed and associated sidings as many an old Yeovilian will fondly remember. The date is about 1955. However, the sad view, below, taken around 1973, will bring tears to the eyes of any inveterate 'train-spotter'. Such wanton destruction – all for the sake of a now under-used car park.

HORSE-OMNIBUS, SOUTH STREET, c. 1880. Horse-omnibuses used to regularly ply their trade between the town's railway stations and the principal hostelries (see p.28). This 'carte-de-visite' photograph shows three public houses: the Cow Inn, 7 South Street (run by Thomas Knott, inn-keeper and bricklayer), the Greyhound Hotel, 8 South Street (Robert McAulay, hotel-keeper and auctioneer) and the Globe & Crown, 73 South Street (John Tucker, simply an inn-keeper!). [Gosney photograph]

SOUTH STREET/PETTERS WAY c. 1955. A view of South Street at its junction with what is now the pedestrianised King George Street with Petters Way on the left. The Community Arts Centre at 80 South Street is without it's wall mural and the Baptist church is still enjoying popularity. Built on the site of an earlier meeting house of 1668, a chapel was erected in 1810 and replaced 30 years later by a still larger building. The new front and other extensions were subsequently added and finally the Newnam Memorial Hall was built in 1912. Now the subject of much controversy for its dilapidated state, locals await its fate at the hands of developers.

Six

Events

YEOVIL REVIEW, May 1937.

PRESENTATION OF SIDNEY GARDENS FOUNTAIN, 24 May 1899. Amongst those attending the presentation were, left to right (standing): George Henry Gould (1860?-1935), Edward Samuel Ewens, -?-, William Walter Johnson (1853?-1928), George Wrentmore Gawler, James Bazeley Petter (see p.98), Mayor, Councillor John Vincent (1840-1934), William Kaye Lewis Armytage, Mace-bearer Henry Jesty (1854?-1927), Charles John Hook (1855?-1929), John Kerbey Whitby, Henry Francis Raymond, -?-, Miss Farley, William Tanner Maynard. Sitting: Sidney Watts (1833-1918), Miss Watts, Miss Vincent, Mrs Elizabeth Charlotte Christmas Vincent (mayoress), -?-, William Cox (1820-1911), -?-, Joseph Chaffey Moore (1833?-1901), Charles Wreford Pittard (see p.99), Henry Butler Batten (see p.102), John Howe Farley, Ebenezer Pittard (see p.99), Henry Cary Tompkins (1823?-1899), William Beale Collins. The gardens had been given to the town by Councillor Watts, during his mayoralty, in commemoration of Queen Victoria's 'diamond jubilee' (1897). They had been formally opened, complete with bandstand donated by Councillor Petter, on 23 June 1898. This ornamental fountain (recently restored), provided by Mr Farley, was the finishing touch to this three-acre public park.

Opposite: CORONATION DECORATIONS, 13-15 SOUTH STREET, Summer 1902. The coronation of Edward VII (1841-1910) was originally set for 26 June 1902, but only two days before it had to be postponed until 9 August, on account of an attack of appendicitis which required an emergency operation. To the left of the heavily decorated house, can be seen the business premises of Frederick Cridland (1856-1927), builder – and subsequently captain of the Yeovil Volunteer Fire Brigade (see p.46) and an alderman.

KING LEWANIKA AT THE MANSION HOUSE, 42 KINGSTON, 5 June 1902. Amongst those present at the reception were, left to right (standing): Herbert William Southcombe (1859-1944), John Greenwell Raymond, -?-, John Kerbey Whitby, James Bernard Paynter, Dr Edward Charles Garland, John Howe Farley, -?-, Colonel Colin Harding (1863-1939), -?-, William Walter Johnson (1853?-1928), George Henry Gould (1860?-1935), Henry Francis Raymond, -?-, -?-, Edmund Damon (see p.100), William Cox (1820-1911). Sitting: 'Johnny', Lewanika (1842?-1916) – King of Barotseland (now Zambia), Mayor, Alderman Sidney Watts (1833-1918), Judge Frederick Adolphus Philbrick (1836-1910). The King was in Britain to attend the coronation of Edward VII (1841-1910).

GOLD TORQUE INQUEST, 18 August 1909. 'A golden torque [seen below], ascribed to the middle Bronze Age, was found about the 25 May 1909, in Mr Chapman's garden on Hendford Hill, Yeovil, owned by Messrs. Bird & Pippard. It was found on the earth, after digging, by Henry Cole, of Yeovil, gardener. The owner thereof cannot now be known. There is no evidence that it has ever been in ancient times hidden or otherwise concealed'. Such was the verdict of the 'treasure trove' inquest (seen above), held at Yeovil Town Hall, under the jurisdiction of Coroner Edward Queckett Louch (1857-1943). The torque, weighing over five ounces, had previously been purchased from Mr Cole, for £40 plus half its additional value (if any) – by the Somerset Archaeological and Natural History Society. Its secretary, Harold St. George Gray (1872-1963), had strongly resisted any attempts to deprive them of it and so it remains in the Somerset County Museum, Taunton, to this day!

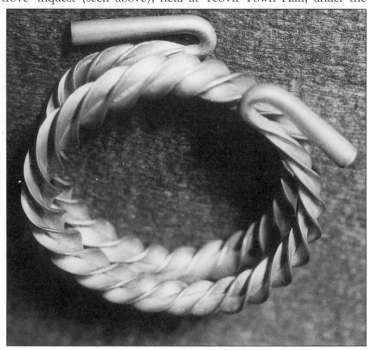

PROCLAMATION OF GEORGE V, 9 May 1910. A wonderfully evocative shot of Edwardian Yeovil, taken in the Borough. The death of Edward VII (1841-1910) ended the reign of one of the best-known and most popular of British Kings; so long awaited and so short lived, 1901-1910.

CORONATION OF GEORGE V, 22 June 1911. A year later children and spectators in St. John's churchyard heard the official announcement of the new monarch's Coronation. George V (1865-1936) was the second son of Edward VII. He served in the navy until 1892, when on the death of his brother, he became heir to the throne. He reigned from 1910 -1936. The Mayor at the time was Edmund Damon (see p.100).

PEACE DAY, 19 JULY 1919. This date was designated for peace celebrations across Great Britain and her Empire 'so grievously hurt by the Great War of 1914-18'. Yeovil's thanksgiving service was held in Wyndham Fields. The top photograph shows the 'Peace Mayor' Councillor Mitchelmore, (see p. 101) noticeable with his chain of office, on his left is the mace bearer Henry Jesty (1854?-1927). The Rev.Herbert Ceceil Sydenham vicar of Yeovil is seen wearing his canonicals. Following the service abouT 700 ex-servicemen marched through the town, behind the Yeovil Town Band, to a civic reception in one of the large hangers at the Westland works. The bottom photograph shows the marchers in lower Middle Strret, passing the Liberal Club on the right (not visible in this photograph).

OPENING OF THE BATH & WEST SHOW, BARWICK PARK, 25 May 1932. Amongst the Yeovil Town Council delegation were, left to right: Joseph George Boucher (mace-bearer), Major (later Colonel) Batten (town clerk, see p.102), Mayor, Alderman William Earle Tucker (1864-1956), Alderman Mitchelmore (see p.101), Deputy Mayor, Councillor Sidney Charles Clothier (1877-1947), Alderman Jabez Matthews (1857?-1935). This four-day agricultural show, organised by the Bath & West & Southern Counties Society (the 'Royal' came much later), attracted almost 45,000 visitors.

ROYAL VISIT AT THE BATH & WEST SHOW, BARWICK PARK, 27 May 1932. The Prince of Wales, later Edward VIII (1894-1972), centre right, can be seen inspecting the guard of honour, formed by 120 Legionaries of Somerset and Dorset, shortly after his arrival at the showground. Accompanying him is Colonel Frank Davidson Urwick (1874-1936), president of the Yeovil branch of the British Legion (again, the 'Royal' came later). After lunch, the Prince addressed a crowd of nearly 20,000 people and candidly observed that 'sometimes we are too individualistic and go on producing types of commodities no longer generally suited to the present-day requirements' (*Western Gazette*) – sounds like a prophecy of the EC grain and butter 'mountains'!

MAYPOLE DANCING AT BRAGG CHURCH *c.* 1930. The Church of England Fayre at Bragg Church, Hendford Hill, was always a popular event. The fayre took place every year courtesy of John Vincent (1840-1934) Mayor of Yeovil 1898-1901. He used to readily lend the beautiful grounds of Bragg Church, his home, for public functions for charitable purposes.

SATURDAY MORNING CINEMA CLUB AT THE ODEON, 1947. The Saturday morning cinema club audience was made up local boys and girls who would gather each week to watch a cartoon, a serial and a feature film. Seats downstairs were 6d (2.5 p) and 9d (4 p) in the balcony. Discipline was maintained by teenage boys and girls. It was not unusual for the balcony occupants to bombard the main auditorium with assorted missiles. The Odeon Cinema opened in 1937 when 'patrons' were assured 'that in all the 1,700 seats, perfect reproduction will be enjoyed in absolute comfort'!

INAUGURATION OF A30 TRUNK ROAD LIGHTING, 29 July 1949. This nocturnal photograph of the Mayor Benjamin Dening (1889?-1954) and others was taken at the opening of Yeovil's trunk road lighting scheme. From left to right: Alderman S.H. Vincent (Chairman of Public Lighting Committee), His Worship the Mayor, Colonel H.C.C. Batten (Town Clerk) (see p.102), the Mayoress, Mr. T.S. Jewels (Deputy Town Clerk), Mr R. Harding (Borough Treasurer), Mr A.J. Price (Borough Surveyor), Mr E.D.G. Hiscott (Chief Committee Clerk and Mayor's Secretary), Mrs D.V. Vincent (Councillor).

PROCLAMATION OF ELIZABETH II, 8 February 1952. The bombed Medical Hall (Boots) is seen at the back of this civic procession. The bomb damage was eventually cleared and Burger King now occupies the site. The Mayor was Stanley Howard Vincent (1893?-1975) and the Town Clerk Thomas Sheraton Jewels (1915-1986). Proclamations were attended by large numbers of people and schools took their pupils to witness the historic event.

'CORONATION' STREET PARTY, 2 JUNE 1953. Local people celebrated Queen Elizabeth II's Coronation with street parties. Unfortunately the weather forced many party-goers indoors. This photograph shows the local children of North Terrace and Eastland Road, before the party started.

YEOVIL TRADES FAIR, 3 July 1954. Marshal of the Royal Air Force Sir John Cotesworth Slessor (1897-1979) recently retired as Chief of the Air Staff, is seen above arriving at the opening of the Yeovil Trades Fair. The event took place in the grounds of Hendford Manor and was heralded as an enormous success. The Westland Dragonfly G-ALIK (S51 Mk. IA) has a particular niche in the history of Westland Aircraft as it was the first helicopter to be built, under licence, by the company. It was a four-seat general purpose helicopter which made its maiden flight on 5 October 1948.

Seven

Disasters

TOWN HALL BLAZE

—o—

If this had been Your Property would it have been adequately **INSURED**

?

Don't wait until you have to call the Fire Brigade before answering this question.

Prudential policies afford adequate cover against the numerous risks run by House-holders and Shopkeepers.

Obtain full particulars from the Company's local representative or fill in and forward this coupon.

WESTERN GAZETTE, 27 September 1935

CHAPMAN FIRE, MILL LANE, 23 April 1909. 'Disastrous fire at Yeovil' [sic] – so was the headline from the *Western Gazette*. The fire broke out in the range of buildings adjoining the old Town Mill, and also destroyed premises occupied by Messrs. Chapman & Co., Builders, Ebenezer Pittard (see p.99), leather dresser and a cottage occupied by a certain Frederick Masters. Other buildings and their contents used by Messrs. Ewens & Johnson, glove manufacturers for storing leather dressings were also badly damaged. The total cost of the damage was stated to be nearly £10,000, the majority £7,000 being Ewens & Johnson's loss; 30 men employed at the various works were made unemployed by the disaster. Visible in the background of the bottom picture is the gas works (see p.19).

APLIN & BARRETT FIRE, NEWTON ROAD, 11 August 1912. Two members of the London Fire Brigade who were on holiday in Yeovil at the time, assisted the directors and other local fire fighters in containing the fire at the premises of Messrs. Aplin & Barrett and St. Ivel Ltd. At one point the fire, watched by thousands of onlookers took hold, and threatened to engulf a new range of buildings adjoining Wyndham Fields. The report from the *Western Gazette*, stated that these buildings contained 'new and valuable machinery and a very large stock of a most inflammable character'. It does not say what the stock consisted of but thanks to the relentless efforts of local Fire Brigades, including that of Sherborne, the flames were confined to a single wing of the building, mainly office accommodation and part of the creamery. The damage was estimated at between £15,000 to £20,000.

PEN MILL RAILWAY ACCIDENT, 8 August 1913. It is somewhat surprising that there has been only one major railway accident involving loss of life in the Yeovil area. This occurred when the Paddington–Weymouth express, headed by *City of Bath* (GWR 4-4-0 No.3710), ploughed into the back of a stationary excursion train at Pen Mill. Three passengers died and nine were injured. At the subsequent inquest, a verdict of accidental death through the momentary distraction of the driver's attention (and not of culpable negligence) was recorded. Ironically, the *City of Bath* had achieved some fame ten years earlier, by breaking a world speed record on its non-stop journey between Paddington and Plymouth.

YEOVIL JUNCTION RAILWAY ACCIDENT, 4 July 1914. This accident happened as a result of an Exeter–Salisbury goods train, unintentionally slipping its couplings as it sped through Sutton Bingham. Avoiding action was being taken when the two sections of the train collided just west of Yeovil Junction. Though involving no loss of life, the smash de-railed and wrecked about 20 goods trucks. It also demolished the West signal box – the signalman narrowly escaping with his life.

TOWN HALL FIRE, HIGH STREET, 22 September 1935. In 1830 the Town Commissioners joined with the old Yeovil Corporation and set about removing the old Market House and the shambles from the Borough. They also commissioned the building of a Town Hall, and on 20 June 1849 it was opened. Later a tower was built to take a combination of clock and bells, striking the hour and quarters, but this was found to be unsafe and removed in 1887. In 1913 a new tower was erected but this time an eleborate steel construction distributed the weight between the four walls; the clock had four dials each about six feet in diameter and the top of the turret was nearly 100 feet above the pavement. The fire which destroyed the Town Hall was discovered at about twenty to four on the Sunday morning. Smoke was seen rising from the ventilators under the clock tower and within minutes it was ablaze. The thousands of pounds worth of damage included the loss of two paintings, which hung in the Council Chamber. The building was completely gutted.

BUS CRASH, HORSEY LANE, 9 January 1953. Seven people were injured when this Southern National double-decker bus, carrying shoppers and work people to their homes around lunchtime, crashed through railings and came to rest above the stream at the Hendford end of Horsey Lane. The bus was precariously balanced at a 45 degree angle against a wall in the yard adjoining the offices of Messrs. Burt and Son. Ltd. with its nearside wheels and exit overhanging a shallow stream which runs alongside the road. Ladders were used to extricate the passengers through the emergency exit on the top deck. Work to bring the bus upright did not begin until later that evening when two five-ton cranes, from depots at Weymouth and Taunton, had arrived on the scene.

FLOODING AT STARS LANE, December 1972. These two pictures of the floods at Dodham Brook illustrate how vulnerable that area was to flooding. The 'No Cycling' sign in the top photograph is rendered superfluous by the sheer volume of standing water. The other sign, referring to a visitors car park, was for the firm of C.J. (Yeovil) Ltd., precision casters whose premises were located at the bottom of Stars Lane. Reminders of the disused Town Station (see p66-67) are apparent in both pictures. The old engine shed in the back of the top picture is a stark reminder of the effects of the Beeching 'axe'. The bottom print shows Dodham Bridge spanning the old Yeovil to Taunton line at the foot of Summerhouse Hill. The old mill, on the right, is now let as individual business units.

Eight

School-Days

WHITBY'S ALMANACK, 1891

YEOVIL COUNTY SCHOOL, KINGSTON, *c.* 1910. Founded in 1845 by John Aldridge (1813?-1892), the school settled on this site five years later. The original Kingston School had occupied only the imposing, shuttered building on the right – the former home of Martock-born, sanitary reformer, Dr Thomas Southwood Smith (1788-1861). Somerset County Council took over the running of the school, in 1905, and subsequently greatly enlarged it. Known then as Yeovil County School, it changed its name (yet again) to Yeovil School in 1925 – apparently on a whim of the headmaster.

GOVERNORS AND MASTERS, YEOVIL COUNTY SCHOOL, *c.* 1909. Back row, left to right: Charles John Hook (1855?-1929), -?-, -?-, -?-, -?-. Middle: -?-, -?-, John Reid, -?-, Dr William Alfred Hunt (1845-1929), -?-, -?-, Dr Ptolemy Augustus Colmer (1867-1931), -?-, Frank Chadd Rudd (headmaster), -?-, George Henry Gould (1860?-1935), -?-, Frank Edgar Bastick (music master), -?-, Ebenezer Pittard (see p.99). Front: John Vincent (1840-1934), -?-, -?-, -?-, John Henry Boll (see p.100), Henry Stiby (see p.2), Mayor, Alderman William Cole (1851-1910), -?-, -?-, Levi Beer, Edmund Damon (see p.100), Norman Buchanan (see p.101), Herbert William Southcombe (1859-1944). [Stiby photograph]

OPENING OF HUISH ELEMENTARY SCHOOL, 6 October 1905. This junior school was built at a cost of £5,000, on three-quarters of an acre in the Huish recreation field, and housed 300 infants and 250 girls. The Mayor (Henry Stiby) and Corporation opened the school amidst much civic pride. In his speech the Mayor stressed that greater prominence should be given to subjects 'like hygiene and domestic economy, so that girls could grow up to be of use to their mothers and when in after life they became wives and mothers they would become the centre of a happy and well ordered home.'

HUISH ELEMENTARY SCHOOL, c. 1928. Back row, left to right: -?-, -?-, Joyce Langham, -?-, -?-, Joan Sly. Second row: Elsie Rowe, -?-, Betty Welsh, Olive Hayward. Third row: -?-, -?-, -?-, -?-, Ethel Webber, -?-, -?-. Fourth row: -?-, -?-, -?-, -?-, Alice Stidson, -?-, Freda Fisher. Front: Janie Marsh, May Baker, Queenie Hawkins. At this time Miss Annie Gillies was the girls' mistress and Miss May Noble was in charge of the infants. (Perhaps someone might be able to supply the missing names?).

RECKLEFORD ELEMENTARY SCHOOL, 1928. Back row, left to right: ? Sims, Kenneth Bird, Jack Way, Wreford Sartin, Jack Cousins, Sid Jeffery, Phil Eason, Percy Day, Fred Matthews, Charlie Strode, Reg Jeffery. Second row: Mr Edward A Stagg (headmaster), John Norman, Fred Wareham, Norman Windsor, Les Higgins, Jack Featherstone, ? Norris, John Harris, Kenny Dodge. Third row: 'Patch' Peaty, Harold Gill, Alec McDonald, Eddie White, Mervyn Mitchell, Mr Brown (gardening teacher), Harold Phillips, Roy Pearce, Vic Tavener, ? Wright, Kenny Chapman. Front: Harry Ridout, Fred Bishop, Sid Heathcote, Victor Hockey, Ken Sibley, Roland Davis, Hugh Gardner, Gordon Hosie, Fred Moore, Eric Bolton, Stanley Parsons. Originally opened as Yeovil's first Board School in 1876, it could accommodate 250 boys and 216 girls.

STAFF OF GRASS ROYAL SECONDARY SCHOOL, July 1947. Back row, left to right: J.M'L. Pugh, R.H. Crocker, W.H. Young, C.T. Davies, W.H. Henderson. Middle row: R.T. MacMillan, M. Felix, E.M. Hunt, M.L. Porter, O.G. Eden, N. Stubbs, J.M. Hall. Front: J.G. Mitchem, E.M. Challice, Edward A. Stagg (headmaster), F.E. Price, W.A. Taylor. Opened in 1939, Mr Stagg had transferred as head from Reckleford (see above photograph) to Pen Mill and eventually to Grass Royal. It is now a junior school.

Nine

Pastimes

THE 'FACILE'

SAFETY

BICYCLE.

PRICE LISTS

On application to the

SOLE AGENT for YEOVIL

And Neighbourhood,

J. H. BOLL,

AT

Hill's Carriage Works,

YEOVIL.

YEOVIL VOLUNTEER BAND, *c.* 1880. Standing, left to right: Alfred Dunn, Ebenezer Giles, Harry Pomeroy, Walter Bond, Herbert Jenner, Alfred Beare (bandmaster), William Fort, Jack Fort, Charles Lane, E.J. Lucas. Sitting: George Larcombe, Walter Creese, Albert Ostler, Herbert Slade, -?-. Bandmaster Beare was a beer retailer at 54 Huish (known as the 'Bee Hive'). Having been in charge since the band was reformed, in 1870, he finally lay his baton down after some 26 years' service. The band was attached to 'F' Company, Second Volunteer Battalion, Prince Albert's Somersetshire Light Infantry, based at the Armoury, Ram Park (now the Armoury public house, 1 The Park).

ST. JOHN THE BAPTIST CHURCH CHOIR, 1906. Back row, left to right: W. May, ? Jones, ? Feld, ? Grinter, ? Miles, Walter Wesley Legg, -?-. Middle row: ? Battishall, R. Mitchell, ? Rendall, ? Palmer, Hubert Henry Holwill, C.J. Hayne, ? Spring, ? Rodway, Dr Charles James Marsh (1856-1940), Gus Smith, John Goodchild (see p.97), -?-, -?-, -?-, -?-, -?-, -?-, -?-. Front: -?-, -?-, E. Moyle, -?-, E. Mitchell, ? Naish, Frank Edgar Bastick (organist), Rev Preb James Phelips (1852-1930), Rev Thomas Rowland Winterton (curate), -?-, -?-, -?-, -?-. Though actually born at Cucklington, near Wincanton, Prebendary Phelips was a member of the well-known Montacute family (see p.118). He was Vicar of Yeovil, 1898-1911.

HOLY TRINITY SCOUT GROUP, 1928. Among those thought to be present are Cubs: N. Dover, R. Edmunds, H. Goodland, Rob Griffin, Les Higgins, R. Mapledorum, F. Robbins, Heber Rowe, Ken Sibley, Eddie White, Cyril Willmott, F. Winsor. Scouts: Eric Bolton, J. Clements, H. Dover, Reg Edmunds, E. Elliott, Wally Elliott, Stanley Fry, R. Giles, Lewis Gregory, R. Gundry, Douglas Harris, Dennis Hart, J. Jennings, A. Patten, Leonard Pitcher, Fred Ricketts, Stanley Ricketts, Aubrey Whensley. Rovers: Roy Dover, W. Giles, A. Horsey, T. Horsey, F. McGarry, P. Patten, Ray Penney, Walter Priddle, Rowland Whensley. This was the oldest scout group in Yeovil, having been formed in 1918.

EDWARD DYER AND HIS PIANO ACCORDION BAND, 1932. Left to right: Ernie Turner, Edward Dyer (bandleader), Barbara Hallett, Fred Matthews, Wreford Sartin, Lionel Abbott, Ron Wellman. 'DA' on the drums stood for 'Dyer's Accordians' (later changed to 'ED' – 'Ed Dyer's'), who became well-known locally, playing at venues such as the Odeon (now MGM) Cinema (see p.78). The band broke up at the commencement of the Second World War, with its leader joining the Military Police.

YEOVIL TOWN FOOTBALL CLUB, 1949. Back row, left to right: Stan Abbot, Jerry Gardener, Joe Langford, Bert Gosney, Dick White, Arthur Lamb. Second row: -?-, Jack Ray, Graham Whensley, Hedley Cook, Dennis Harrison, Eric Bryant, Stan Hall, Dickie Dyke, Les Blizzard, -?-, -?-, -?-, Reg Rogers, Stan Swinfen. Seated: Henry Merrilt. Ralph Davis, Dave Afflick, Arthur Hickman, Bill Farthing, H. A. Smith (Chairman), Alec Stock, Nick Collins, Ray Wright, Jackie Hargreaves. Front row: -?-, ? Black, Ken Whitlock, Ken Hayward, Bobby Hamilton, -?-. Yeovil and Petters United was formed in 1908 as a combination of two teams already established – the Town's team and Petters United who had a ground in Brickyard Lane. In 1921 the Club moved to Huish where they played for the next seventy years before selling the site to Tesco and relocating to the Huish Park Stadium on the outskirts of town.

Ten

Personalities

WHITBY'S ALMANACK, 1882

WALTER RAYMOND (1852-1931), *c.* 1920. The son of a glover, author Walter Raymond ('Tom Cobleigh') was born in the Vicarage Street house shown below. Educated at Kingston School (see p.88), in adulthood he shunned his father's business and set out on a literary career that would produce over twenty volumes of novels, essays and plays. As a regional novelist he is often compared (usually unfavourably!) with Thomas Hardy (see p.24) and it is known that the two did correspond. Amongst his better known published works are: *Gentleman Upcott's Daughter* (1893), *Tryphena in Love* (1895), *The Book of Simple Delights* (1906) and the semi-autobiographical *Under the Spreading Chestnut Tree* (1928). His dialect play *Two Men o'Mendip* (1898/1924) was performed at London's Cripplegate Theatre in 1929. Mr Raymond loved the Somerset countryside ('Ciderland') and wrote towards the end of his long life: 'It was in consequence of a misfortune that I was born in a town, but my heart was always in the fields and with the folk'. During the inter-war years he was an ardent supported of the 'Somerset Folk Movement'. Following his death a commemorative plaque was erected in the old Yeovil Library, which has since been transferred to the new premises.

JOINT-PROPRIETORS OF THE *WESTERN GAZETTE, c.* 1880. On the left sits Charles Tite (1842-1933), the former owner of the rival *Western Flying Post*, which had amalgamated with the *Western Gazette* in 1867. At his death he bequeathed to the Corporation of Yeovil a substantial number of his antiquarian books – these now form the nucleus of Yeovil Library's local history collection. His partner, Charles Clinker (1835?-1886), originally founded the *Western Gazette* in a rented cottage in Brunswick Street in 1863. Tragically, he died of a heart attack, alone, in the basement of a London hotel – shortly after completing an important business deal.

JOHN GOODCHILD (1878-1957), *c.* 1939. Born at Cowley, Middlesex, John Goodchild came to Yeovil in 1906 as a reporter on the *Western Gazette*. Subsequently promoted to chief reporter, during the First World War he went to France as a war correspondent, experiencing several narrow escapes! From 1922-1951 he served as editor of the paper. Keenly interested in local history and archaeology he accepted the Town Council's invitation, in 1954, to compile a centenary history of the modern Corporation. In this he was ably assisted by Leonard Charles Hayward (1906-1992), History Master at Yeovil School (see p.88) and Ernest Arnold Batty, Borough Librarian and Curator (see p.102). His son, John Newis Goodchild (1913-1993), also served as editor of the *Gazette* between 1966-1978 – quite a family achievement!

THE PETTER FAMILY OF YEOVIL, 1895. Aboard their own 'horseless carriage' are, left to right: James Bazeley Petter (1846-1906), Percival Waddams Petter (1873-1955), Herbert William Southcombe (1859-1944), Ernest Willoughby Petter (1873-1954). The twins, Ernest and Percy, designed and built the one horse-power engine themselves (now displayed in the Museum of South Somerset) and the vehicle body was constructed by Hill & Boll (see p.100). When asked by a local landowner how their cars were doing, one of the brothers replied 'we are still pushing them'. Back came the facetious response 'you usually are when I see you'! The Grange, 18 The Park, below, was the Petter family home for many years. It was demolished in 1976 to make way for the Queensway dual-carriageway.

THE CARD FAMILY OF YEOVIL
c. 1900. The family house, originally
numbered 19 Hendford (later
renumbered 51), was home and
business to the Card family of tailors.
Established early in the nineteenth-
century by Ephraim Card his son
George for many years a Yeovil
councillor, took over the business in
1900 and ran it for 39 years. George's
sisters Lottie and Evalina Card ran
the Dorothy Cafe in South Street
until 1955 and another brother
Albert carried on the tailors business
in Hendford until the early 1950s.
The house was scheduled for
demolition in the mid 1960s but is
seen here with Albert and his father
George Jonas Minty Card on the
front path.

EBENEZER PITTARD (1847-1929),
c. 1920. Born in a house on lower
Middle Street, Ebenezer and his
brother, Charles Wreford Pittard
(1844-1912), succeeded to the family
leather business upon the death of
their father (Charles) in 1867. The
brothers eventually went their
separate ways, with Ebenezer
establishing his own dressing yard at
the bottom of Mill Lane. He was
long-associated with elementary
education in the town, serving on the
Yeovil School Board (and its
successors) from 1880-1920. Made a
Freeman of the Borough in 1926, at
the same time that Henry Stiby (see
p.2) was honoured, he also gave life-
long devotion to the South Street
Baptist Church Sunday School (see
p.22). A teacher there for 50 years, in
his younger days he had walked many
miles to preach the gospel in village
chapels!

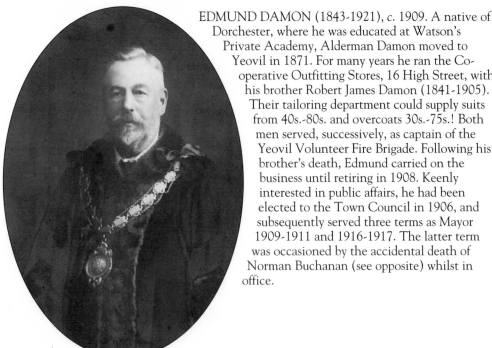

EDMUND DAMON (1843-1921), c. 1909. A native of Dorchester, where he was educated at Watson's Private Academy, Alderman Damon moved to Yeovil in 1871. For many years he ran the Co-operative Outfitting Stores, 16 High Street, with his brother Robert James Damon (1841-1905). Their tailoring department could supply suits from 40s.-80s. and overcoats 30s.-75s.! Both men served, successively, as captain of the Yeovil Volunteer Fire Brigade. Following his brother's death, Edmund carried on the business until retiring in 1908. Keenly interested in public affairs, he had been elected to the Town Council in 1906, and subsequently served three terms as Mayor 1909-1911 and 1916-1917. The latter term was occasioned by the accidental death of Norman Buchanan (see opposite) whilst in office.

JOHN HENRY BOLL (1858-1916), c. 1911. The descendant of an old Hanoverian (German) family of shipowners and corn merchants, Alderman Boll settled in Yeovil in 1878 – becoming a naturalised British subject seven years later. After marrying his employer's daughter (Bessie), he eventually succeeded to the headship of the firm of Hill & Boll, Park Road. This was the coach builders who assisted Petters in the construction of their 'horseless carriage' in 1895 (see p.98). Elected to the Town Council in 1898, he served as Mayor 1911-1912, the highlight of his term being the inauguration of the Council's first large housing estate at New Town. Somewhat ironically, during the First World War he released many of his employees to join the 'Colours' and at the time of his death, his only son (Frederick), was away at the Front fighting his former-compatriots!

NORMAN BUCHANAN (1857-1916), *c*. 1912. Born on the Isle of Lewis, in the Outer Hebrides, Councillor Buchanan arrived in Yeovil in 1880 to pursue the drapery trade. With his business successfully established at 10 Sherborne Road, he was elected to the Town Coucnil in 1906. Greatly interested in educational matters, he was one of the Council's representatives on the Yeovil County School board of management (see p.88). He served four terms as Mayor 1912-1916, towards the end of which his duties increased considerably on account of chairing all the numerous 'war committees' that had sprung up. Tragically, he was the first Mayor to die 'in harness', as a direct result of injuries sustained in falling downstairs at his home, Osborne House, Sherborne Road – on New Year's Eve!

WILLIAM RICHARD EDWARDS MITCHELMORE (1863-1939), *c*. 1912. A Devonian by birth, Alderman Mitchelmore and his wife (Ellen) came to Yeovil in 1895 to run temperance (i.e. non-alcoholic) hotels: the Albany (see p.19) and later the Fernleigh (see p.20). He was elected to the Town Council in 1907, and subsequently became the 'Peace Mayor', serving three terms 1918-1921. A keen advocate of municipal housing, Mitchemore Road was named in his honour. He was also an enthusiastic antiquarian, undertaking preliminary investigations at the Westland Roman villa site in 1925. The Wyndham Museum (now the Museum of South Somerset), opened in 1928 to display the Roman 'finds', was largely due to his exertions. Appropriately, he was made its first honorary curator, and in 1930 a Freeman of the Borough. For many years he chaired the Education Committee and in the week before his death (which occurred at the Municipal Offices), he had participated in the opening of two new schools: Grass Royal (see p.90) and Summerleaze Park.

HERBERT COPELAND CARY BATTEN (1884-1963), *c.* 1912. Colonel Batten was the third generation of his family to successively hold the office of Town Clerk of Yeovil. His grandfather, John Batten (1815-1900), was the first occupant 1854-1876; to be followed by his uncle, Henry Butler Batten (1845-1912), serving 1876-1912 and finally Herbert himself 1912-1949 – something of a record! During the First World War he served with the Dorsetshire Regiment, being mentioned in despatches several times, and was awarded the DSO. The Second World War found 'The Colonel' (as he was invariably known), organising the local detachment of the Home Guard (see p,46). Created a Freeman of the Borough in 1949, his family law firm – Batten & Co., Church House – continues to this day.

ERNEST ARNOLD BATTY (1908-1985), *c.* 1955. A face no doubt familiar to many of the older generation of Yeovilians, Mr Batty was appointed Borough Librarian and Assistant Curator in 1935 – on the princely salary of £225! He (and Yeovil) hit the headlines during the 1950s, when the 'white spot for purity' campaign was launched in Yeovil Library, at the behest of a councillor who feared that the public was being shocked by pornographic literature. The campaign, however, was short-lived! A founder-member of the Yeovil Archaeological and Local History Society, in 1954, the same year he co-authored a history of the Borough (see p.97). Retiring in 1969, he moved first to Axminster and subsequently settled in Bridport where he died. (The bookshelves in the background conveniently help to date this photograph!).

Eleven

...and Around

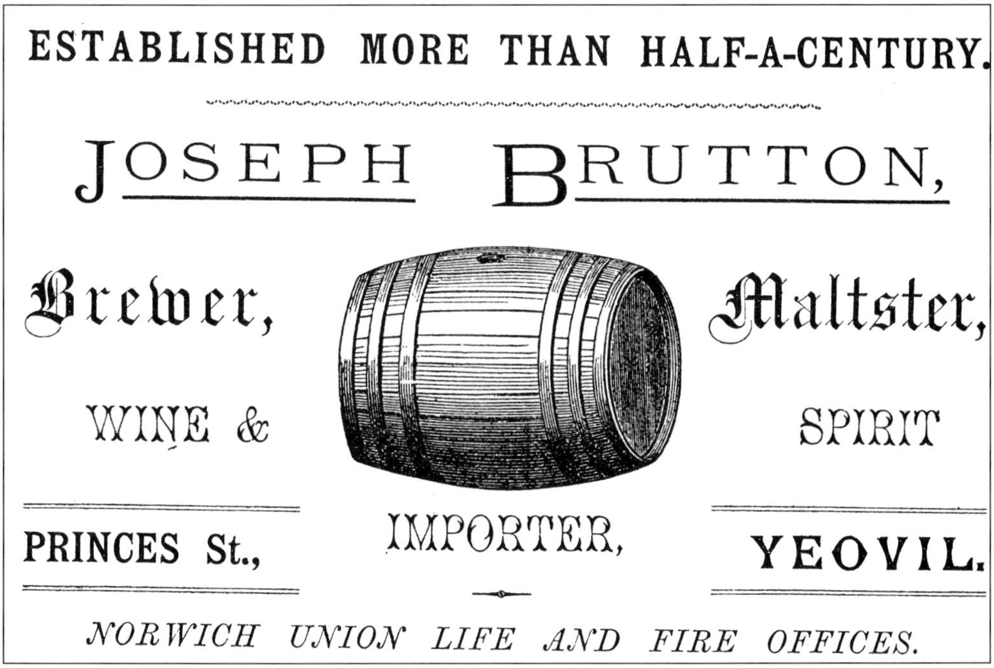

ESTABLISHED MORE THAN HALF-A-CENTURY.

JOSEPH BRUTTON,

𝕭𝖗𝖊𝖜𝖊𝖗, 𝕸𝖆𝖑𝖙𝖘𝖙𝖊𝖗,

WINE & SPIRIT

PRINCES St., IMPORTER, YEOVIL.

NORWICH UNION LIFE AND FIRE OFFICES.

WHITBY'S ALMANACK, 1881.

BARWICK PARISH CHURCH (ST. MARY MAGDALENE), *c.* 1880. This ancient church, standing proud above the surrounding sandstone 'hollow-ways' (sunken lanes), is basically of the fifteenth-century. Inside there are wonderfully carved bench-ends of 1533, depicting various rural scenes: a man climbing a tree and dogs chasing a rabbit. The churchyard contains several graves relating to the Batten family (see p.102), of nearby Aldon House. Parish registers survive from 1560 and are now deposited at the Somerset Record Office, Taunton. [Stiby photograph]

BARWICK HOUSE, *c.* 1875. The house probably dates from the late eighteenth-century, but underwent a drastic 'face-lift' in the early years of the nineteenth. It successively provided a home to the Newman and Messiter families, served as an American army base during the Second World War, subsequently a Borstal detention centre, and finally, has recently been converted into luxury apartments. Behind Barwick House there is an elaborate grotto, which complements the four follies found scattered around the estate (see opposite) [Gosney photograph]

BARWICK PARK FOLLIES, *c.* 1885. Mystery still surrounds the origins of these four extraordinary rubble follies, two of which are illustrated here. Right is the 'Rose Tower' and below, 'Jack the Treacle-Eater'. The latter gained its fanciful name after a supposed treacle-eating, fleet-footed messenger (Jack), who it is said used to run to London for the local landowner (how he fared in the capital's marathon is not recorded!).

Construction of the follies has been variously attributed to the Newman family in the late eighteenth-century and the Messiters in the early nineteenth. Local tradition alleges that some of them at least, were built to alleviate unemployment, during a particularly severe recession in the gloving industry. The identities of the figures in the photographs are not known. [Stiby photographs]

BRYMPTON PARISH CHURCH (ST. ANDREW), *c.* 1885. Dating largely from the fifteenth-century, the most striking external feature of this church is its over-sized bellcot. The interior contains a vast array of medieval monuments to lords of the manor. To the left can be seen the early sixteenth-century west front of Brympton House. Parish registers survive from 1699 and are now deposited at the Somerset Record Office. [Stiby photograph]

THE PONSONBY-FANE FAMILY OF BRYMPTON, 7 October 1897. Standing are, left to right: Anitha Ponsonby, Robert Ponsonby, Mary Ponsonby, Edmund R. Turton, Clementina Turton, Richard Ponsonby, John Ponsonby, Rt. Hon. Sir Spencer Cecil Brabazon Ponsonby-Fane (1824-1915), Sydney Ponsonby, William Phelips, Theobald Ponsonby, Hugh Ponsonby. Sitting: Florence Ponsonby, Edmund J. Turton, Margaret de Grey, Violet Ponsonby, Hon. Lady Lousia Anne Rose Ponsonby-Fane (1825-1902), Marjorie Phelips, Constance Phelips, Pat Ponsonby, Audrey Ponsonby, Clare Phelips, Bertha Ponsonby. The family is assembled outside the seventeenth-century, south front, of Brympton House (their home) to celebrate Sir Spencer and Lady Louisa's 'golden' wedding anniversary.

CHILTHORNE DOMER PARISH CHURCH (ST. MARY THE VIRGIN), 19 September 1883. The building is mainly of the fourteenth-century, with a dominant western bellcot somewhat reminiscent of Ashington and Brympton (see opposite). At first glance it resembles a small fortification, rather than a church, such is the profusion of battlements along the nave roof and gables! Inside there is a recumbent effigy of a knight, dated about 1275, belonging either to the Domer or Vagg families. Parish registers survive from 1678 and are now deposited at the Somerset Record Office, Taunton. [Stiby photograph]

CHILTHORNE DOMER SCHOOL, 1925. This Church of England village school was opened in 1871 for 91 children. The school mistress at about this time was Mrs Hannah Nicholson.

EAST STREET, CREWKERNE *c.* 1900. The rather unusual name 'Crewkerne' derives from 'Cruc' being an old British word for hill and 'aern' a house or store house. Its market was recorded in the Domesday book of 1086 as being the second most valuable in Somerset. The bow-fronted shop, fourth on the left, was the original post office and 'Saunder' the chemist first on the left.

VICTORIA HALL, CREWKERNE, *c.* 1915. Two very dashing First World War soldiers pose outside the Victoria Hall with their Douglas motor cycles. On the right of the picture is a local man Lieutenant James William Symonds, who features in the following photograph as a younger man. Today the Victoria Hall has been completely refurbished and is the new Community Office as well as the Town Hall.

JAMES WILLIAM SYMONDS. Corporal James William Symonds was driver to General Sir Arthur Henry Fitzroy Paget (1851-1928), General Officer Commanding Aldershot District, 1903 to 1906. He is seen at the wheel of a Panhard-Lavassor which he drove while stationed at Aldershot. He was a highly respected soldier who rose through the ranks to gain a Commission, retiring as a major in 1933.

CREWKERNE STATION. Crewkerne station opened in 1861 when the population of the town was only about 4,500. Although nearer to the village of Misterton it is on the main London (Waterloo) to Exeter line. In 1906 the northern siding extended through a gate into Bradford's coal yard and the cramped goods yard was, until the 1930s, shunted by a horse.

EAST COKER PARISH CHURCH (ST MICHAEL), *c.* 1885. Recent investigations have indicated that parts of this church may be Saxon in origin. Inside there are commemorative plaques to Captain William Dampier (1651-1715), 'buccaneer, explorer, hydrographer' and Thomas Stearns Eliot (1888-1965), the American-born British poet and playwright – whose ashes were returned to East Coker, the home of his paternal ancestors. Parish registers survive from 1560 and are now deposited at the Somerset Record Office. [Stiby photograph]

THE FOOT FAMILY OF EAST COKER, 1907. Left to right: Florence Foot, John 'Jack' (1874?-1958), Frederick John (1895?-1927), in front, Frank (1901-1988), Sarah Ellen (1872?-1952), Lucy. This 'classic' rural scene of the gamekeeper, with his gun, dog and family was photographed at the keeper's cottage, on Lodge Hill, East Coker. 'Jack' Foot was employed on the Coker Court estate and was a renowned shot. His son Frank, in adulthood, manually wound the clock of the parish church, every night, for 60 years!

CHARLES POWELL (1843-1923), *c.* 1916. Born in Abergavenny, Monmouthshire, the Reverend Powell was ordained a priest in Exeter in 1872. Following the curacies of Churchstow and West Alvington, Devon, he came to East Coker in 1877 and remained vicar until 1921. Always interested in village life, he founded the cricket club (sadly recently disbanded), the reading-room and the bell-ringing team (which he captained for many years). He also found time to compile *Notes about East Coker* (1910) and delve into the life of Dampier (see opposite). In the photograph, taken on the vicarage verandah (since removed), Reverend Powell is flanked by two of his daughters and Stanley Stevens (home from the First World War).

EAST COKER BAND, *c.* 1900. Back row, left to right: Percy Francis, Jim Boucher, S. Hooper, R. Rendell, G. Rendell, A. Rendell, E. Baker, N. Pitcher. Front: Tom Neville, E. Gillham, T. Sibly (conductor), H. Rendell, Frank Rendell, T. Lawrence. This brass band was founded by George Troyte-Chafyn-Grove (1829-1913), of North Coker House, in January 1897. Its first engagement was five months later at the local celebrations for Queen Victoria's 'diamond jubilee'. During the Boer War it combined with the Crewkern Military Band, to raise money for widows and orphans. (The last surviving member of the band, Percy Francis (1887-1993), was severely wounded during the First World War and taken prisoner. However, he lived to the incredible age of 106!)

THE PRINCE OF WALES, HAM HILL, *c.* 1906. Run by William Taylor, at this time, this nineteenth-century public house has survived all weathers perched high up on top of Ham Hill. The hill was once one of the largest Iron Age hill-forts in Europe, with massive ramparts remaining to prove it. Occupied later by the Romans, they first realised the great potential of the golden limestone (Ham stone) for building purposes. Disused quarries abound, though one is still working, giving the area a distinctive 'moon-scape' appearance! Owned by the Duchy of Cornwall (in effect, the Prince of Wales – hence the pub's name), it is now designated a 'country park' and administered by South Somerset District Council.

HEBDITCH CHILDREN AT HAM HILL, *c.* 1930. Left to right: Geoffrey Francis Hebditch (born 1921), Michael Stanley (born 1927), David Henry (1925-1986), John Alan (born 1919). All of the children belonged to the Hebditch farming family of New Cross, Kingsbury Episcopi (see p.116 and p.117). Note the boy on the left, holding a ball, appears to be wearing hobnailed shoes. It is thought that this cheerful 'band of brothers' was photographed on the west side of Ham Hill, overlooking Norton-sub-Hamdon (see p.121) – still a popular picnic spot, more than half-a-century later.

THE JUKES FAMILY OF HOLTON, *c.* 1905. Left to right: Lucy Jukes, née Foot (1863?-1938), Herbert George (1891?-1976), Walter (1898?-1961), Frank (1856-1933), Frances (1893-1983). This evocative Edwardian 'cabinet portrait' wonderfully captures the Jukes family in their Sunday best. No doubt there was great excitement, especially amongst the children, as they travelled the short distance from Holton to the photographer's studio in Wincanton. Two older daughters were away 'in service' and thus missed this family gathering. The parents, Frank and Lucy, had been married at Mill Street Baptist church, Wincanton, on Christmas Day 1880 – a rare day off work for an agricultural labourer.

HARVEST TIME NEAR HOLTON, *c.* 1910. A typical rural scene in the Holton area (possibly on the Holton House estate), that was once quite common throughout south Somerset – and now only to be nostalgically observed at 'Yesterday's Farming' events! Ironically, the 'stationary' steam engine could only be moved with the assistance of 'real' horse-power, judging by the shafts to the right. The labourer standing on the middle of the steam engine (with cider flagon), confirms that this photograph pre-dates drink-driving legislation! (Note the unusual occupant of the wicker basket in the centre foreground).

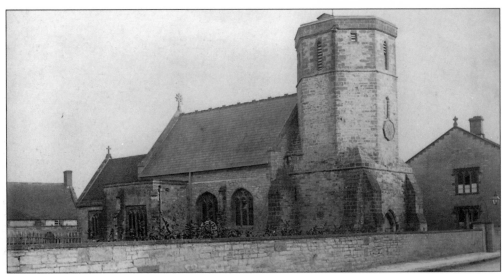

ILCHESTER PARISH CHURCH (ST. MARY MAJOR), *c.* 1885. The town of Ilchester was unique in that during the medieval period it possessed at least six parish churches – St. Mary Major being the sole survivor! Largely of the thirteenth-century, its massive octagonal tower (similar to Barrington, Somerton and South Petherton), was nicely mirrored by the octagonal clock-face (since removed). Inside the south aisle is a brass memorial commemorating Ilchester's famous son, Roger Bacon (1214?-1292), the philosopher and experimental scientist who is often erroneously credited with the invention of gunpowder. Parish registers survive from 1690 and are now deposited at the Somerset Record Office. [Stiby photograph]

WEST STREET (now HIGH STREET), ILCHESTER, *c.* 1905. Looking north towards Ilchester Bridge, the site of the medieval gaol was about where the most distant trees are to be seen. In 1599 a new gaol was erected on the north bank of the River Yeo (Ivel), and though enlarged several times it was often so over-crowded that some prisoners had to be housed in the town! After complaints of brutality the gaol finally closed in 1843, the inmates being transferred to Wilton Gaol, Taunton. During the period of its existence, the gaol effectively made Ilchester the county town of Somerset.

WILLIAM DAVID HENRY ARMSTRONG (1855-1925), *c.* 1900. Born in Victoria, Australia, the Reverend Armstrong was ordained a priest in London in 1883. Following curacies in Fulham and Hammersmith, he came to Ilchester in 1889 and remained rector until 1912. Whilst a member of the Yeovil Rural District Council, he interested himself in housing and sanitary matters, being an enthusiastic supporter of any schemes that promoted public health. His last parish was Berrow, 1912-1917, from which living he resigned on account of a serious breakdown in health. Unfortunately, he never recovered and died at Burnham-on-Sea some eight years later.

VEEL'S ALMSHOUSE INMATES AND FRIENDS, ILCHESTER, *c.* 1900. Back row, left to right: Job Goff, -?-, -?-, John Cox. Middle: Samuel Dunford, Samuel Cox, Marina Pope, Elizabeth Huxtable, Elizabeth Bennett, Keziah Masters, Richard Ivey, Samuel Hallett. Front: -?-, Bessie Snook, -?-, rector's children. The boy is believed to be Edward William Armstrong (1892?-1915). Whilst serving as a Second Lieutenant with the Rifle Brigade, during the First World War, he was mortally wounded. Veel's Almshouse was originally founded in 1426 for twelve men. By the time of this photograph, women had been admitted, and inmates were being provided with 'clothing, fire, medical attendance and four shillings per week'!

THORNEY ROAD, KINGSBURY EPISCOPI, *c.* 1910. Looking towards the centre of the village, the new Wesleyan Methodist church, opened in 1900, is standing tall in the far distance. Peeping over the roof-tops, at the right, is the highly-ornate, Ham stone tower belonging to the parish church of St. Martin. The solitary cyclist seems about to set off down the road that leads, eventually, to Martock. Kingsbury Episcopi comprises numerous scattered settlements, including East Lambrook, Mid Lambrook, West Lambrook, Stembridge and New Cross.

NEW CROSS, KINGSBURY EPISCOPI, *c.* 1930. An aerial view of New Cross, where the Hebditch family have farmed continuously for over a century – and are still going strong! Over the years this interesting complex of buildings has also been home to a steam-powered iron foundry and a brickworks – the latter supplying bricks for the construction of Horn Hill (road) tunnel, near Beaminster, opened in 1832. The farmhouse, foreground left, was apparently moved from South Petherton, in the mid nineteenth-century, brick-by-brick. Unfortunately, the chimney and large barn, were both destroyed by fire around 1970.

THE HEBDITCH FAMILY OF NEW CROSS, KINGSBURY EPISCOPI. Outside New Cross (above) in the wagonette, around 1928, are left to right: -?-, Geoffrey, David, Michael, Emma Hebditch, née Vaux (1859-1947). Standing is the boys' father, William Henry (1896-1975). The latter is also shown below, around 1900, with his own father another William Henry Hebditch (1857-1917), astride a fine-looking horse called 'Kitty'. (Family history is truly brought alive by photographs such as these.)

MIDDLE STREET, MONTACUTE *c.* 1910. St. Michael's Hill overlooks the Ham stone village of Montacute and in this postcard, the sixteenth-century west tower of St. Catherine's church stands out above the village. The road leads down to the Kings Arms, visible at the end of the street.

THE KINGS ARMS, MONTACUTE *c.* 1885. Built in the later part of the 1700s, the Kings Arms is still unchanged today. Montacute lies to the west of Yeovil and is home to one of the grandest National Trust properties in England. Montacute House was built in the late sixteenth-century by Sir Edward Phelips (1560?-1614); its long gallery is unique and houses an outstanding collection of Tudor and Stuart portraits – on loan from the National Portrait Gallery. [Stiby photograph]

PRIORY GATEHOUSE, MONTACUTE, *c.* 1885. This early sixteenth-century gatehouse, is all that survives from the Cluniac priory, founded around 1102. The two towers, either side of the gateway, are stair-turrets. However, the tower, on the extreme right, belongs to the parish church of St Catherine. The vicar at this time was the Reverend Charles Francis Powys (1843-1923) – three of who's eleven children (!) were destined to achieve a degree of literary fame: John Cowper (1872-1963), Theodore Francis (1875-1953) and Llewelyn (1884-1939). [Stiby photograph]

ROYAL VISIT TO MONTACUTE HOUSE, 11 June 1932. 'Old-world picturesqueness and West Country loveliness mingled in a wonderful setting, with Montacute House one of the most beautiful of Elizabethan mansions, as its background' – so the *Western Gazette* gushingly described the visit of the Princess Royal (1897-1965), only daughter of George V. As commandant-in-chief of the British Red Cross Society's Voluntary Aid Detachments (VAD), she inspected 700 members of the Somerset branch. Subsequently, the Princess formally handed over the title-deeds of Montacute House to the chairman of the National Trust.

MAIN STREET, MUDFORD c. 1920. Mudford village is situated north-east of Yeovil and divided by the A359 which slices it in two. The Half Moon is advertising the local beer while the little boy outside is perhaps waiting for the delivery man. Founded by Joseph Brutton (1831-1914) Bruttons brewery (see p. 163) was on Princes Street in Yeovil and could trace its origins back to 1825. The square building next door to the pub was a skittle alley before it was knocked down and replaced by chalets in the 1980s.

THE WEIR, MUDFORD c. 1920. This postcard view taken seventy years ago shows a scene little changed from today, still popular with local fishermen, its position on the River Yeo (Ivel) makes it both accessible and attractive. The weir appears on the Ordnance Survey map of 1889 which reveals at least two weirs established at that time. Mudford means "muddy ford" and the sunken lane beside the parish church still has flood-warning signs in evidence.

NORTON-SUB-HAMDON PARISH CHURCH (ST. MARY THE VIRGIN), *c.* 1885. Described by one cleryman-historian as being 'of almost feminine gracefulness; tall, narrow, and beautifully proportioned' (!) this early sixteenth-century church, built of the local Ham stone, is a superb example of Perpendicular architecture. The circular dovecot at the foot of the tower, is all that remains of the original manor house. To the right of the church can be seen the National School, erected in 1842 (now a local authority primary school). Parish registers survive from 1558 and are now deposited at the Somerset Record Office. [Stiby photograph]

HIGHER STREET, NORTON-SUB-HAMDON, *c.* 1898. This picturesque, seventeenth-century, Ham stone dwelling (now called Shepherds Cottage), has since exchanged its thatch for clay tiles. On the photographer's side of the 'kissing-gate' is 'Blackbarrow' – a common field in which a considerable quantity of Roman remains (pottery, bones and a denarius) were found in May 1897. Note the Victorian nesting-box on the gable end. This photograph was first published in *Norton-sub-Hamdon* (1898), by local-born Charles Trask (1830-1907).

ST. JAMES'S STREET, SOUTH PETHERTON, *c.* 1880. Looking along St James's Street towards the fourteenth-century cottages, behind the boys, that were demolished in 1911 to make way for the William Blake Memorial Hall. Built 'for the furtherance of the Liberal cause' it was vehemently opposed, even by the Somerset Archaeological and Natural History Society! The covered wagon, just beyond Joseph Henry Anstice's bakery, looks more reminiscent of the 'Wild West' than the South-West.

THE BELL INN (later BREWER'S ARMS), ST JAMES'S STREET, 1924. When the thatched roof of his public house caught fire, licensee Gilbert Gunn had a problem on his hands. Fortunately, Captain Thomas Walter and the men of the South Petherton Volunteer Fire Brigade, were soon on the scene to put out the conflagration. The pub was rebuilt in the following year. No doubt, forever afterwards, the boys in the foreground wanted to grow up to be firemen!

THE HARDING FAMILY OF SOUTH
PETHERTON. The contented-looking
couple, right, are Francis Ebenezer Harding
(1868-1943) and his wife Elizabeth Ellen
Harding, née Anstice (1864?-1936). Francis
was employed as a solicitor's clerk, with
Hugh R. Poole & Son, St James's Street,
from the age of twelve until he retired! The
photograph was taken in 1928 at Rock
House, Palmer Street – the birthplace of
their illustrious son, seen below. Captain
(later Field-Marshal) Allan Francis 'John'
Harding (1896-1989), is pictured here with
his nephew, Geoffrey Hebditch (see p.112)
at New Cross, Kingsbury Episcopi (see
p.116 and p.117) in 1925. The Harding and
Hebditch families were related by marriage.
'John' Harding distinguished himself in
both World Wars, winning the MC in the
First, and being knighted in the field by
George VI (1895-1952) during the Second.
He was ennobled in 1948, becoming Chief
of the Imperial General Staff some four
years later.

STOKE CROSS, STOKE-SUB-HAMDON *c.* 1900. An early postcard of Stoke-sub-Hamdon published by A.W. Chant, and post marked 1906. Nestling beneath the steep sides of Ham Hill, West and East Stoke comprise the parish of Stoke-sub-Hamdon. The place was well known for its Ham stone quarries and by the early eighteenth-century was a noted centre for the gloving trade.

LIBERAL DEMONSTRATION, STOKE-SUB-HAMDON *c.* 1910. An unusual photograph of a Liberal demonstration going up towards Ham Hill. From 1872 George Mitchell of Montacute organised annual open air rallies in support of a national agricultural workers' union. Ham Hill was, from then on, a popular venue for political and trades unions demonstrations.

SUTTON BINGHAM PARISH CHURCH (ALL SAINTS), *c.* 1885. This jewel of a church, seating no more that 50, and dating from the Norman period, was reputedly consecrated in the year 1111. It possesses a superb chancel arch and in the churchyard there stands the remains of a fourteenth-century sepulchral cross (to the left of the railings). However, its crowning glory are the medieval wall paintings, discovered in 1868 and 1917. Most of the parish now lies submerged under 40 feet of water – see below for explanation! Parish registers survive from 1742 and are now deposited at the Somerset Record Office, Taunton. [Stiby photograph]

CONSTRUCTION OF SUTTON BINGHAM RESERVOIR, 1953. Building work on the reservoir and dam began in 1951 and was completed some four years later. Financed by the Yeovil Rural District Council, the final cost was just under £1 million. The earth-fill dam, whose exit can be seen above, was 1,045 feet long, 44 feet high, and was constructed from materials excavated on site. The reservoir-capacity was 575 million gallons. In addition to drinking-water, it now provides a home to a variety of wildfowl and the Sutton Bingham Sailing Club.

TINTINHULL PARISH CHURCH (ST. MARGARET), 16 April 1883. Largely of the early thirteenth-century, surviving church records allow the porch to be dated 1441-1442 and the top of the tower (including projecting stair-turret) to 1516-1517. The wooden louvre panels, covering the bell-openings, have since been removed. Parish registers survive from 1561 and are now deposited at the Somerset Record Office. [Stiby photograph]

TINTINHULL GLOVE FACTORY c. 1880. Gloving began in Tintinhull as far back as 1327, when the names John Glover and John Le Scynner appeared in a lay subsidy roll. An even earlier record of 1265 shows that the rent paid for forty acres of land at Tintinhull was one pair of gloves of the value of one penny; the tenant being one Christina, daughter of Eustace the Carpenter. This photograph of Southcombe glove factory was taken before the firm acquired the business of Thomas Ensor and Sons of Milborne Port in 1895. 5th from left, back row (hat and beard) – George Hillard. 4th from right, back row – Tom Hayward. 2nd from left, back row – Harry Russell. 4th from left seated – Tom Read. 2nd from left seated – Willie Warner. 1st and 2nd from right, standing – Tom and Joe Tavener. 1st from right sitting – Dick Pullen.

FRANCIS FARM, TINTINHULL *c.* 1900. A charming photograph of an early traction engine up to steam, taken at Francis Farm in the early 1900's. Tom Francis is standing and Glen is standing on the tow hitch with Joe Francis in the driving seat. The farm was built in 1784 by their ancestor Hugh Francis.

COOKERY CLASS, TINTINHULL *c.* 1920. The parish of Tintinhull straddles the Roman Foss Way (A303) just to the South West of Ilchester. These teenage girls from local schools had congregated together for a cookery class. Whether the class had finished or was about to begin we cannot tell, but by the look of the bowls and towels laundry may well have formed part of the days lesson.

EAST STREET, WEST COKER, *c.* 1900. Looking south-east, with the entrance to Manor Street on the left, towards Job Gould's West of England Twine Works (obscured by the cottages). The most distant cottage was the old bakery. West Coker was famous for its growing of flax and hemp for sailcloth manufacture, and 'Coker canvas' was highly esteemed by the navy during the Napoleonic Wars.

MANOR HOUSE, WEST COKER, *c.* 1894. Rebuilt in the late fifteenth-century, following its destruction during the Wars of the Roses, this beautiful Ham stone house is located (appropriately) on Manor Street. The porch, seen in the centre, is dated 1600 and over successive centuries the building has been much altered and extended. Long-owned by the Portman family, of Orchard Portman, it was purchased in 1907 by Sir Matthew Nathan (1862-1939), a retired colonial diplomat. He wrote the scholarly *Annals of West Coker* (1957) – published posthumously. This photograph was first published in *Historical and Topographical Collections relating to ... South Somerset* (1894), by John Batten (see p.102).

Stock List

(Titles are listed according to the pre-1974 county boundaries)

BERKSHIRE

Wantage
Irene Hancock
ISBN 0-7524-0146 7

CARDIGANSHIRE

Aberaeron and Mid Ceredigion
William Howells
ISBN 0-7524-0106-8

CHESHIRE

Ashton-under-Lyne and Mossley
Alice Lock
ISBN 0-7524-0164-5

Around Bebington
Pat O'Brien
ISBN 0-7524-0121-1

Crewe
Brian Edge
ISBN 0-7524-0052-5

Frodsham and Helsby
Frodsham and District Local History Group
ISBN 0-7524-0161-0

Macclesfield Silk
Moira Stevenson and Louanne Collins
ISBN 0-7524-0315 X

Marple
Steve Cliffe
ISBN 0-7524-0316-8

Runcorn
Bert Starkey
ISBN 0-7524-0025-8

Warrington
Janice Hayes
ISBN 0-7524-0040-1

West Kirby to Hoylake
Jim O'Neil
ISBN 0-7524-0024-X

Widnes
Anne Hall and the Widnes Historical Society
ISBN 0-7524-0117-3

CORNWALL

Padstow
Malcolm McCarthy
ISBN 0-7524-0033-9

St Ives Bay
Jonathan Holmes
ISBN 0-7524-0186-6

COUNTY DURHAM

Bishop Auckland
John Land
ISBN 0-7524-0312-5

Around Shildon
Vera Chapman
ISBN 0-7524-0115-7

CUMBERLAND

Carlisle
Dennis Perriam
ISBN 0-7524-0166-1

DERBYSHIRE

Around Alfreton
Alfreton and District Heritage Trust
ISBN 0-7524-0041-X

Barlborough, Clowne, Creswell and Whitwell
Les Yaw
ISBN 0-7524-0031-2

Around Bolsover
Bernard Haigh
ISBN 0-7524-0021-5

Around Derby
Alan Champion and Mark Edworthy
ISBN 0-7524-0020-7

Long Eaton
John Barker
ISBN 0-7524-0110-6

Ripley and Codnor
David Buxton
ISBN 0-7524-0042-8

Shirebrook
Geoff Sadler
ISBN 0-7524-0028-2

Shirebrook: A Second Selection
Geoff Sadler
ISBN 0-7524-0317-6

DEVON

Brixham
Ted Gosling and Lyn Marshall
ISBN 0-7524-0037-1

Around Honiton
Les Berry and Gerald Gosling
ISBN 0-7524-0175-0

Around Newton Abbot
Les Berry and Gerald Gosling
ISBN 0-7524-0027-4

Around Ottery St Mary
Gerald Gosling and Peter Harris
ISBN 0-7524-0030-4

Around Sidmouth
Les Berry and Gerald Gosling
ISBN 0-7524-0137-8

DORSET

Around Uplyme and Lyme Regis
Les Berry and Gerald Gosling
ISBN 0-7524-0044-4

ESSEX

Braintree and Bocking
John and Sandra Adlam and Mark Charlton
ISBN 0-7524-0129-7

Ilford
Ian Dowling and Nick Harris
ISBN 0-7524-0050-9

Ilford: A Second Selection
Ian Dowling and Nick Harris
ISBN 0-7524-0320-6

Saffron Walden
Jean Gumbrell
ISBN 0-7524-0176-9

GLAMORGAN

Around Bridgend
Simon Eckley
ISBN 0-7524-0189-0

Caerphilly
Simon Eckley
ISBN 0-7524-0194-7

Around Kenfig Hill and Pyle
Keith Morgan
ISBN 0-7524-0314-1

The County Borough of Merthyr Tydfil
Carolyn Jacob, Stephen Done and Simon Eckley
ISBN 0-7524-0012-6

Mountain Ash, Penrhiwceiber and Abercynon
Bernard Baldwin and Harry Rogers
ISBN 0-7524-0114-9

Pontypridd
Simon Eckley
ISBN 0-7524-0017-7

Rhondda
Simon Eckley and Emrys Jenkins
ISBN 0-7524-0028-2

Rhondda: A Second Selection
Simon Eckley and Emrys Jenkins
ISBN 0-7524-0308-7

Roath, Splott, and Adamsdown
Roath Local History Society
ISBN 0-7524-0199-8

GLOUCESTERSHIRE

Barnwood, Hucclecote and Brockworth
Alan Sutton
ISBN 0-7524-0000-2

Forest to Severn
Humphrey Phelps
ISBN 0-7524-0008-8

Filton and the Flying Machine
Malcolm Hall
ISBN 0-7524-0171-8

Gloster Aircraft Company
Derek James
ISBN 0-7524-0038-X

The City of Gloucester
Jill Voyce
ISBN 0-7524-0306-0

Around Nailsworth and Minchinhampton from the Conway Collection
Howard Beard
ISBN 0-7524-0048-7

Around Newent
Tim Ward
ISBN 0-7524-0003-7

Stroud: Five Stroud Photographers
Howard Beard, Peter Harris and Wilf Merrett
ISBN 0-7524-0305-2

HAMPSHIRE

Gosport
Ian Edelman
ISBN 0-7524-0300-1

Winchester from the Sollars Collection
John Brimfield
ISBN 0-7524-0173-4

HEREFORDSHIRE

Ross-on-Wye
Tom Rigby and Alan Sutton
ISBN 0-7524-0002-9

HERTFORDSHIRE

Buntingford
Philip Plumb
ISBN 0-7524-0170-X

Hampstead Garden Suburb
Mervyn Miller
ISBN 0-7524-0319-2

Hemel Hempstead
Eve Davis
ISBN 0-7524-0167-X

Letchworth
Mervyn Miller
ISBN 0-7524-0318-4

Welwyn Garden City
Angela Eserin
ISBN 0-7524-0133-5

KENT

Hythe
Joy Melville and Angela Lewis-Johnson
ISBN 0-7524-0169-6

North Thanet Coast
Alan Kay
ISBN 0-7524-0112-2

Shorts Aircraft
Mike Hooks
ISBN 0-7524-0193-9

LANCASHIRE

Lancaster and the Lune Valley
Robert Alston
ISBN 0-7524-0015-0

Morecambe Bay
Robert Alston
ISBN 0-7524-0163-7

Manchester
Peter Stewart
ISBN 0-7524-0103-3

LINCOLNSHIRE

Louth
David Cuppleditch
ISBN 0-7524-0172-6

Stamford
David Gerard
ISBN 0-7524-0309-5

LONDON
(Greater London and Middlesex)

Battersea and Clapham
Patrick Loobey
ISBN 0-7524-0010-X

Canning Town
Howard Bloch and Nick Harris
ISBN 0-7524-0057-6

Chiswick
Carolyn and Peter Hammond
ISBN 0-7524-0001-0

Forest Gate
Nick Harris and Dorcas Sanders
ISBN 0-7524-0049-5

Greenwich
Barbara Ludlow
ISBN 0-7524-0045-2

Highgate and Muswell Hill
Joan Schwitzer and Ken Gay
ISBN 0-7524-0119-X

Islington
Gavin Smith
ISBN 0-7524-0140-8

Lewisham
John Coulter and Barry Olley
ISBN 0-7524-0059-2

Leyton and Leytonstone
Keith Romig and Peter Lawrence
ISBN 0-7524-0158-0

Newham Dockland
Howard Bloch
ISBN 0-7524-0107-6

Norwood
Nicholas Reed
ISBN 0-7524-0147-5

Peckham and Nunhead
John D. Beasley
ISBN 0-7524-0122-X

Piccadilly Circus
David Oxford
ISBN 0-7524-0196-3

Stoke Newington
Gavin Smith
ISBN 0-7524-0159-9

Sydenham and Forest Hill
John Coulter and John Seaman
ISBN 0-7524-0036-3

Wandsworth
Patrick Loobey
ISBN 0-7524-0026-6

Wanstead and Woodford
Ian Dowling and Nick Harris
ISBN 0-7524-0113-0

MONMOUTHSHIRE

Vanished Abergavenny
Frank Olding
ISBN 0-7524-0034-7

Abertillery, Aberbeeg and Llanhilleth
Abertillery and District Museum Society and Simon Eckley
ISBN 0-7524-0134-3

Blaina, Nantyglo and Brynmawr
Trevor Rowson
ISBN 0-7524-0136-X

NORFOLK

North Norfolk
Cliff Richard Temple
ISBN 0-7524-0149-1

NOTTINGHAMSHIRE

Nottingham 1897–1947
Douglas Whitworth
ISBN 0-7524-0157-2

OXFORDSHIRE

Banbury
Tom Rigby
ISBN 0-7524-0013-4

PEMBROKESHIRE

Saundersfoot and Tenby
Ken Daniels
ISBN 0-7524-0192-0

RADNORSHIRE

Llandrindod Wells
Chris Wilson
ISBN 0-7524-0191-2

SHROPSHIRE

Leominster
Eric Turton
ISBN 0-7524-0307-9

Ludlow
David Lloyd
ISBN 0-7524-0155-6

Oswestry
Bernard Mitchell
ISBN 0-7524-0032-0

North Telford: Wellington, Oakengates, and Surrounding Areas
John Powell and Michael A. Vanns
ISBN 0-7524-0124-6

South Telford: Ironbridge Gorge, Madeley, and Dawley
John Powell and Michael A. Vanns
ISBN 0-7524-0125-4

SOMERSET

Bath
Paul De'Ath
ISBN 0-7524-0127-0

Around Yeovil
Robin Ansell and Marion Barnes
ISBN 0-7524-0178-5

STAFFORDSHIRE

Cannock Chase
Sherry Belcher and Mary Mills
ISBN 0-7524-0051-7

Around Cheadle
George Short
ISBN 0-7524-0022-3

The Potteries
Ian Lawley
ISBN 0-7524-0046-0

East Staffordshire
Geoffrey Sowerby and Richard Farman
ISBN 0-7524-0197-1

SUFFOLK

Lowestoft to Southwold
Humphrey Phelps
ISBN 0-7524-0108-4

Walberswick to Felixstowe
Humphrey Phelps
ISBN 0-7524-0109-2

SURREY

Around Camberley
Ken Clarke
ISBN 0-7524-0148-3

Around Cranleigh
Michael Miller
ISBN 0-7524-0143-2

Epsom and Ewell
Richard Essen
ISBN 0-7524-0111-4

Farnham by the Wey
Jean Parratt
ISBN 0-7524-0185-8

Industrious Surrey: Historic Images of the County at Work
Chris Shepheard
ISBN 0-7524-0009-6

Reigate and Redhill
Mary G. Goss
ISBN 0-7524-0179-3

Richmond and Kew
Richard Essen
ISBN 0-7524-0145-9

SUSSEX

Billingshurst
Wendy Lines
ISBN 0-7524-0301-X

WARWICKSHIRE

Central Birmingham 1870–1920
Keith Turner
ISBN 0-7524-0053-3

Old Harborne
Roy Clarke
ISBN 0-7524-0054-1

WILTSHIRE

Malmesbury
Dorothy Barnes
ISBN 0-7524-0177-7

Great Western Swindon
Tim Bryan
ISBN 0-7524-0153-X

Midland and South Western Junction Railway
Mike Barnsley and Brian Bridgeman
ISBN 0-7524-0016-9

WORCESTERSHIRE

Around Malvern
Keith Smith
ISBN 0-7524-0029-0

YORKSHIRE
(EAST RIDING)

Hornsea
G.L. Southwell
ISBN 0-7524-0120-3

YORKSHIRE
(NORTH RIDING)

Northallerton
Vera Chapman
ISBN 0-7524-055-X

Scarborough in the 1970s and 1980s
Richard Percy
ISBN 0-7524-0325-7

YORKSHIRE
(WEST RIDING)

Barnsley
Barnsley Archive Service
ISBN 0-7524-0188-2

Bingley
Bingley and District Local History Society
ISBN 0-7524-0311-7

Bradford
Gary Firth
ISBN 0-7524-0313-3

Castleford
Wakefield Metropolitan District Council
ISBN 0-7524-0047-9

Doncaster
Peter Tuffrey
ISBN 0-7524-0162-9

Harrogate
Malcolm Neesam
ISBN 0-7524-0154-8

Holme Valley
Peter and Iris Bullock
ISBN 0-7524-0139-4

Horsforth
Alan Cockroft and Matthew Young
ISBN 0-7524-0130-0

Knaresborough
Arnold Kellett
ISBN 0-7524-0131-9

Around Leeds
Matthew Young and Dorothy Payne
ISBN 0-7524-0168-8

Penistone
Matthew Young and David Hambleton
ISBN 0-7524-0138-6

**Selby from the William Rawling
Collection**
Matthew Young
ISBN 0-7524-0198-X

Central Sheffield
Martin Olive
ISBN 0-7524-0011-8

Around Stocksbridge
Stocksbridge and District History Society
ISBN 0-7524-0165-3

TRANSPORT

Filton and the Flying Machine
Malcolm Hall
ISBN 0-7524-0171-8

Gloster Aircraft Company
Derek James
ISBN 0-7524-0038-X

Great Western Swindon
Tim Bryan
ISBN 0-7524-0153-X

Midland and South Western Junction Railway
Mike Barnsley and Brian Bridgeman
ISBN 0-7524-0016-9

Shorts Aircraft
Mike Hooks
ISBN 0-7524-0193-9

This stock list shows all titles available in the United Kingdom as at 30 September 1995.

ORDER FORM

The books in this stock list are available from your local bookshop. Alternatively they are available by mail order at a totally inclusive price of £10.00 per copy.

For overseas orders please add the following postage supplement for each copy ordered:

European Union £0.36 (this includes the Republic of Ireland)
Royal Mail Zone 1 (for example, U.S.A. and Canada) £1.96
Royal Mail Zone 2 (for example, Australia and New Zealand) £2.47

Please note that all of these supplements are actual Royal Mail charges with no profit element to the Chalford Publishing Company. Furthermore, as the Air Mail Printed Papers rate applies, we are restricted from enclosing any personal correspondence other than to indicate the senders name.

Payment can be made by cheque, Visa or Mastercard. Please indicate your method of payment on this order form.

If you are not entirely happy with your purchase you may return it within 30 days of receipt for a full refund.

Please send your order to:

The Chalford Publishing Company,
St Mary's Mill,
Chalford,
Stroud,
Gloucestershire
GL6 8NX

This order form should perforate away from the book. However, if you are reluctant to damage the book in any way we are quite happy to accept a photocopy order form or a letter containing the necessary information.

PLEASE WRITE CLEARLY USING BLOCK CAPITALS

Name and address of the person ordering the books listed below:

_____

_____

_____ Post code _____

Please also supply your telephone number in case we have difficulty fully understanding your requirements.   Tel.: _____ - _____

Name and address of where the books are to be despatched to (if different from above):

_____

_____

_____ Post code _____

Please indicate here if you would like to receive future information on books published by the Chalford Publishing Company.

____ Yes, please put me on your mailing list   ____ No, please just send the books ordered below

Title	ISBN	Quantity
....	0-7524-_____-___	_____
....	0-7524-_____-___	_____
....	0-7524-_____-___	_____
....	0-7524-_____-___	_____
....	0-7524-_____-___	_____
	Total number of books	_____

Cost of books delivered in UK = Number of books ordered @ £10 each =£		_____
Overseas postage supplement (if relevant)	=£	_____
TOTAL PAYMENT	=£	_____

Method of Payment   ❑ Cheque   ❑ Visa   ❑ Mastercard   **VISA**

Please make cheques payable to *The Chalford Publishing Company*   **MasterCard**

Name of Card Holder   _____

Card Number ❑❑❑❑❑❑❑❑❑❑❑❑❑❑❑❑❑❑❑❑❑❑

Expiry date ❑❑ / ❑❑

I authorise payment of £_____ from the above card

Signed _____